A Comprehensible Guide to
Controller Area Network

Copperhill Media Corporation

http://www.copperhillmedia.com

A Comprehensible Guide to Controller Area Network

2nd Edition

By Wilfried Voss

Published by

Copperhill Media Corporation

158 Log Plain Road

Greenfield, MA 01301

ISBN-10: 0976511606
ISBN-13: 978-0976511601

Printed in the United States of America

Limit of Liability/Disclaimer of Warranty

158 Log Plain Road
Greenfield, MA 01301

ABOUT THIS BOOK

The main reason to write this book was the lack of good printed English literature on CAN basics, which is somewhat disconcerting considering that the technology was first officially introduced in 1986.

There are three official documents describing the CAN standard, the Bosch CAN Specification Version 2.0, the CiA CAN Specification and ISO 11898. The CiA (CAN-in-Automation) specification is a mere copy of the Bosch document, while ISO 11898-1 is an expanded copy with a more scientific approach. All these documents, more often than not, leave ample room for interpretation of the explained topics by omitting elaborating comments, examples or pictures.

It was surprising to find that some special topics, for instance, the CAN Overload Flag, the Bit Stuffing procedure, Bit Resynchronization, and more, are still insufficiently documented. Other documents did provide interesting details, but were somewhat vague on other topics or, in some rare cases, plain wrong.

Some additional works, originally written in German (due to the origination of the technology) are hurt by poor translation, which in turn has a damaging effect on the readability. There are also a vast amount of web sites that contain information on CAN, but they mostly provide only bits and pieces and, after all, they all have commercial aspects in mind.

This book intends to provide adequate information on Controller Area Network (CAN) paired with readability.

The first three chapters provide an overview of Controller Area Network that will allow the reader to understand the basics of CAN without being overwhelmed by technical details:

1.   Overview
Introduces CAN, refers to the history of CAN, CAN applications.

2.   Main Characteristics
Explains in an overview the CAN message frames, bus access, message broadcasting, message priorities, data length and baud rate, bus arbitration and error handling.

3. Benefits of using CAN

Describes the various benefits such as low cost implementation, speed, reliability, error-resistance and worldwide acceptance.

The heart of this book is represented, however, by chapters 4 through 9, which provide more detailed technical insights:

4. Message Frames

Explains the detailed architecture of message frames.

5. Message Broadcasting

Explains the message broadcasting mechanism in a CAN network.

6. Bus Arbitration

Explains the bus arbitration principle in a CAN network.

7. Data Transfer Synchronization

Explains the data transfer synchronization mechanisms between nodes in a CAN network.

8. Error Detection and Fault Confinement

Explains how errors in a CAN network are detected, the determination of sporadic and permanent failures, the fault confinement and error recovery.

9. Physical Layer

Explains the CAN bus medium, bus topology, bus level, bus connections and bus length considerations.

Various technical information in this book is based on the International Standard ISO 11898-1 - Road vehicles – Controller area network CAN) – Part 1: Data link layer and physical signaling and Part 2: High-speed medium access unit

This book does not cover part 3 (Low-speed, fault-tolerant, medium dependent interface) or part 4 (Time-triggered communication) of the ISO 11898 CAN specification, since applications covered by this subject may only apply to automobiles. This book, besides automobile technologies, tries to include industrial automation aspects.

Higher layer protocols based on CAN, such as CANopen, DeviceNet, and SAE J1939 are mentioned briefly, but a more detailed description is not in the scope of this book.

There is already a standard work on **CANopen**: *Embedded Networking with CAN and CANopen* by Olaf Pfeiffer, Andrew Ayre, and Christian Keydel. For further information, refer to http://www.copperhillmedia.com.

The **DeviceNet** Specification, consisting of two volumes: Volume One - Common Industrial Protocol (CIP) and Volume Three- DeviceNet Adaptation of CIP, is available only for ODVA (Open DeviceNet Vendor Association) members. For further information, refer to http://www.odva.org.

The Society of Automotive Engineers (SAE) Truck and Bus Control and Communications Subcommittee has developed a family of standards concerning the design and use of devices that transmit electronic signals and control information among vehicle components. The **SAE J1939** Standards Collection can be found exclusively on the Web at http://www.sae.org.

For more literature on SAE J1939 see also *A Comprehensible Guide to J1939* by Wilfried Voss (http://www.copperhillmedia.com/J1939Book.html).

Note: This second edition of *A Comprehensible Guide to Controller Area Network* does not differ significantly from the first edition as far as the actual content is concerned. The publisher has merely changed the format (and the cover) to improve the print quality of the book.

ABOUT THE AUTHOR

Wilfried Voss is the President of esd electronics, Inc., a company specializing in CAN technology. The company is located in Greenfield, Massachusetts. Mr. Voss has worked in the CAN industry since 1997 and before that was a specialist in the paper industry. He has a master's degree in electrical engineering from the University of Wuppertal in Germany.

Mr. Voss has conducted numerous seminars on CAN and CANopen during various *Real Time Embedded And Computing Conferences* (RTECC), ISA (Instrumentation, Systems, and Automation Society) conferences and various other events all over the United States and Canada. He is also the founder of Copperhill Technologies, a software engineering and consulting company, and the creator of VisualSizer, a comprehensive motor sizing software.

Mr. Voss has traveled the world extensively, settling in New England in 1989. He presently lives in an old farmhouse in Greenfield, Massachusetts with his Irish-American wife, their son Patrick and their Rhodesian Ridgeback.

ACKNOWLEDGEMENTS BY THE AUTHOR

This book would not have been possible without the help of my wife, Dr. Susan Marie Voss, a vigorous proof reader and source of many inspirations.

A great deal of gratitude shall be attributed to the Boston Red Sox, World Series Champions of 2004 & 2007. Go Sox!

TABLE OF CONTENTS

Chapter

1

OVERVIEW

Really! You don't need to know how CAN works...

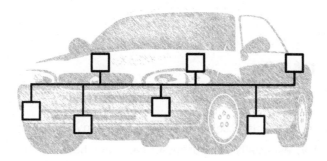

For the longest time the major misconception about Controller Area Network (CAN) was that it is merely used in automobiles. The truth is, CAN, since its introduction in 1986, proved to be a robust, simple and versatile technology and, consequently, CAN found its way into all areas of applications where microprocessors need to communicate among each other.

Along with its undeniable use in automobiles, CAN applications do not only include industrial automation tasks, but any application where distributed control is advantageous and/or a serial bus system will eliminate excessive wiring. CAN proved to be superior to any other field-bus system in regards to low cost, the ability to function in a difficult electrical environment, a high degree of real time capability, excellent error detection and fault confinement capabilities and, almost contradictive to the previously mentioned features, ease of use.

Nowadays there is no special niche for CAN; its use is universal from any industrial application, space and aviation, maritime, medical, down to household appliances such as washers, dryers and even coffee machines.

The ease of use is especially evident for the software engineer who is responsible for the development of a CAN based application. As a matter of fact, the actual CAN protocol, i.e. the entire data communication management including bus arbitration, error detection and fault confinement, etc., etc., is implemented into silicon. CAN controllers know per default what to do and how to do it.

The software engineer is 'demoted' to serve only the basic functions such as initialization, reading data, writing data, checking status and, as a result, to concentrate merely on the actual application software.

This book is intended for those who are not willing to serve the unknown or those who are curious enough to find out why Controller Area Network is so easy to use and yet so extremely reliable.

1.1 WHAT IS CAN?

Controller Area Network (CAN) is a serial network technology that was originally designed for the automotive industry, especially for European cars, but has also become a popular bus in industrial automation as well as other applications. The CAN bus is primarily used in embedded systems, and as its name implies, is a network technology that provides fast communication among microcontrollers up to real-time requirements, eliminating the need for the much more expensive and complex technology of a Dual-Ported RAM.

CAN is a two-wire, half duplex, high-speed network system, that is far superior to conventional serial technologies such as RS232 in regards to functionality and reliability and yet CAN implementations are more cost effective. While, for instance, TCP/IP is designed for the transport of large data amounts, CAN is designed for real-time requirements and with its 1 MBit/sec baud rate can easily beat a 100 MBit/sec TCP/IP connection when it comes to short reaction times, timely error detection, quick error recovery and error repair.

Many major semiconductor manufacturers, such as Motorola, Philips, Intel, Infineon, and many more, sell CAN chips, and the fact that millions of them are used in automobiles guarantees low chip prices and long-term availability. Most semiconductor manufacturers who usually integrated a UART with their microprocessor design, in order to support serial communication for RS 232/485, nowadays tend to integrate CAN instead.

The use of CAN in most European passenger cars and the decision by truck and off-road vehicle manufacturers to use CAN led to the availability of CAN chips since 1987. Other high volume markets, such as domestic appliances and industrial control, also increase the CAN sales figures and guarantee the availability for the future.

CAN networks can be used as an embedded communication system for microcontrollers as well as an open communication system for intelligent devices. Some users, for example in the field of medical engineering, opted for CAN because they have to meet particularly stringent safety requirements.

Similar requirements had to be considered by manufacturers of other equipment with very high safety or reliability requirements (e.g. robots, lifts and transportation systems).

Controller Area Network
- Is a high-integrity serial data communications bus for real-time applications
- Is more cost effective than any other serial bus system including RS232 and TCP/IP
- Provides better ease of use than any other serial bus system
- Operates at data rates of up to 1 Megabit per second
- Has excellent error detection and fault confinement capabilities
- Has the ability to function in difficult electrical environments
- Is now being used in many other industrial automation and control applications
- Is an international standard: ISO 11898

1.2 A BRIEF HISTORY OF CAN

The idea of Controller Area Network (CAN) was hatched by engineers at the Robert Bosch GmbH in Germany in the early 1980s. They investigated the market for a suitable field-bus technology for use in automobiles that would enable them to add further functionality. The main focus was a communication system between a number of ECUs (electronic control units) in vehicles by Mercedes-Benz.

Any field-bus system that is based on serial communication will reduce wiring, which was originally considered only as an advantageous side effect. Distributed control, i.e. the use of a multi-processor system, will consequently result in increased performance and the vastly reduced costs of microcontroller chips in the market already made the use of multiple processors in one system affordable. Other advantages are increased reliability and improved service and maintenance features.

However, none of the existing communication protocols did meet the specific requirements for communication speed and data reliability; as a result they had to develop their own standard.

The involvement of a vehicle manufacturer - Mercedes-Benz- and a semiconductor manufacturer – Intel - as well as several universities in Germany has helped to make CAN a success story.

The CAN standard was first introduced 1986 during the SAE congress in Detroit, Michigan. The first CAN controller chips, the Intel 82526 and the Philips 82C200, were introduced in 1987.

Since then many other semiconductor manufacturers made a decision to produce stand-alone CAN controllers or implement them into their single-chip designs.

Hear Ye! Hear Ye!

The CAN protocol is protected by patents granted to Robert Bosch GmbH. Bosch will grant licenses to manufacturers and universities. For more detailed information about licenses and royalties refer to http://www.can.bosch.com/content/License.html. No CAN license is required for CAN applications based on CAN devices from a licensed manufacturer.

Another crucial milestone for the success of CAN was the establishment of CAN-in-Automation (CiA) in 1992. CiA is the international users' and manufacturers' organization, whose activities are based on members' interest, participation and initiative.

The following table provides an overview of a few milestones in the development and establishment of the CAN protocol[1]:

1983	Start of the Bosch internal project to develop an in-vehicle network
1986	Official introduction of the CAN protocol
1987	First CAN controller chips available from Intel and Philips Semiconductor
1991	Bosch publishes CAN specification 2.0
1992	CAN in Automation (CiA) established as the international users and manufacturers group
1992	CAN Application Layer (CAL) protocol published by CiA
1992	First cars by Mercedes-Benz are being equipped with CAN
1993	ISO 11898 standard published
1994	First International CAN Conference (iCC) organized by CiA
1994	DeviceNet protocol introduced by Allen-Bradley
1995	ISO 11898 amendment (extended frame format) published
1995	CANopen protocol published by CiA

Table 1.2.1: A brief history of CAN

At the present time, the automotive and vehicle industries still dominate the sales of CAN controllers and single-chip controllers with integrated CAN controller at a margin of about 80% to 20% for other applications. The 20% portion represents numerous applications in various non-automotive markets.

---

[1] Source: CAN-in-Automation

Number of Million CAN nodes used all over the world[2]:

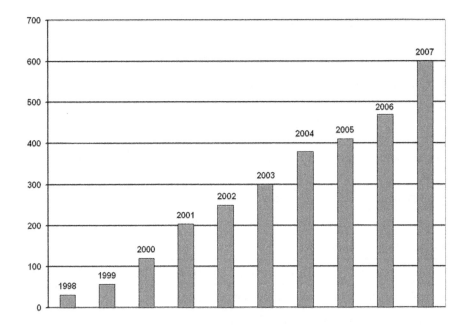

Picture 1.2.1: Number of Million CAN nodes used over time

This brief history of CAN also explains the dominance of German companies in the CAN field, at least as far as the number of CAN businesses can be an indicator for dominance. The CAN technology and especially CAN based higher layer protocols such as CANopen, DeviceNet, and J1939 are increasingly accepted and utilized all over North America, which in turn means that dominance will not result in dependency.

1.3 CAN APPLICATIONS

One frequently asked question is regarding any other field of application, besides automobiles, where CAN is successfully used. As a matter of fact, there is not just one answer, but many. There is no special niche for CAN; its use is universal from any industrial application, space

---

[2] Source: CAN-in-Automation

and aviation, maritime, medicine, down to household applications such as washers, dryers and even coffee machines.

The main advantage of a fieldbus system like CAN lies in the reduction of expensive and maintenance intensive wiring and in the increased performance of a multi-processor system (distributed intelligence). CAN is especially suited to be the serial communication system of choice when excellent performance is a must.

The main applications for CAN are in the fields of

- Passenger Cars
- Trucks and Buses
- Off-Road Vehicles
- Passenger and Cargo Trains
- Maritime Electronics
- Aircraft and Aerospace Electronics
- Factory Automation
- Industrial Machine Control
- Building Automation
- Lifts and Escalators
- Medical Equipment and Devices
- And many more...

Hear Ye! Hear Ye!

Most industrial applications are using higher layer protocols such as CANopen or DeviceNet on top of the CAN application layer (see also Chapter 3.5 - Higher Layer Protocols). It is estimated that about 90% of industrial applications using CANopen do involve at least in part motion control.

Cisco Systems, a networking company, uses a CAN sub-network to implement system initialization and hot-swapping on the large PC boards that implement routers. The number of installed CAN nodes, between 500,000 and 1 million, makes this one of the larger non-automotive applications.[3]

Some other reputable high-tech companies using CAN for various purposes and products are, for instance, Hewlett-Packard, Lockheed, Boeing, NASA, and many more.

Another important market for CAN (in combination with CANopen) is medical equipment and devices, starting from operating room components such as lights and tables, cameras, X-Ray, ultrasound machines, and more, up to larger equipment such as CAT scanners. All major medical companies in the US including GE Medical, Philips Medical and Siemens Medical favor CAN/CANopen over any other fieldbus technology and consequently demand CAN/CANopen compatibility from their numerous vendors and suppliers.

DeviceNet, the other popular higher layer protocol for industrial automation, is especially suited for factory automation and is widely used in the chemical and semi-conductor (wafer handlers and other robotic machinery) industry.

Let's do a case study: One of the most demanding automation tasks in terms of speed and accuracy is motion control. The connection between the control processor (e.g. an industrial PC) with integrated motion controller and the motor with integrated resolver or encoder requires extensive wiring. The situation quickly becomes worse when the task requires the use of multiple motion axes. Not only can the number of wires easily go into the thousands, it also becomes increasingly difficult to add more motion controllers, since, for instance, a PC can only accommodate a certain number of interface boards. Another worsening factor is that each PC's performance will be limited at some point when it comes to reaction times that are necessary to serve each motion controller.

[3] Source: CAN: Network for Thousands of Applications Outside Automotive by Jack Shandle. http://www.techonline.com/community/ed_resource/feature_article/26037

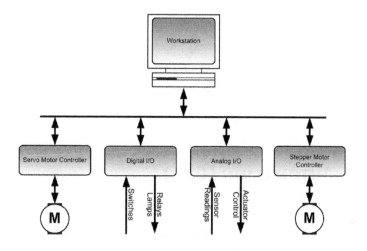

Picture 1.3.1: Sample CANopen Network

The solution to this dilemma is the use of distributed control as shown in an example in picture 1.3.1. Each component, digital and analog I/O, and each motion axis is equipped with its own controller. The network connection between all components and the main controller is accomplished with CAN, in this case actually CANopen. CANopen is a higher layer protocol; an additional software on top of the CAN physical and data link layer (refer to *Chapter 3.5: Higher Layer Protocols*).

This design provides the ease of adding almost unlimited components (CANopen is limited to 128 nodes, which is sufficient for the vast majority of automation applications) without performance loss. The number of wires between the components is reduced to two, which not only reduces the cost of the wiring itself, but also reduces time consuming maintenance and service during start up of the machine or in the case of malfunctions.

The servicing of each component in the network will be improved due to the fact that the engineer only needs to plug the service unit (e.g. a notebook computer) somewhere into the network in order to communicate with either unit. This can be done with only one service software package, since all nodes in the network speak the same language. There is no need for a dedicated service program for each individual unit.

The cost saving resulting from the reduced wiring should not be underestimated. To demonstrate this in the following: A manufacturer in the Boston area produces machinery requiring in average 3 to 5 motion control axes per machine and several hundred I/O points. They overhauled the machine design by using CANopen technologies instead of regular wiring. The cost savings were in the neighborhood of $1,500 per machine. In good economic times they sell 500 machines per year. You do the math...

1.4 CAN-IN-AUTOMATION (CiA)

"CAN in Automation (CiA) is the international users' and manufacturers' organization that develops and supports CAN Standards and CAN-based higher-layer protocols. All activities are based on CiA members' interest, participation and initiative. CiA representatives actively support international standardization of CAN protocols and represent the members' interest in national and international standardization committees, such as ISO and IEC. CiA members initiate and develop specifications that are then published as CiA standards. These specifications cover physical layer definitions as well as application layer and device profile descriptions."[4]

1.5 INTERNATIONAL STANDARD ISO 11898

ISO (the International Organization for Standardization) is a worldwide federation. As its name implies, ISO provides international standards which are prepared and drafted by technical committees. Each member of the ISO, who is interested in the subject for whom a technical committee has been established, has the right to participate in the process of standardization of the corresponding subject.

The ISO 11898 standard, titled "Road vehicles – Controller area network (CAN), was first published in 1993, followed in 1995 by an amendment that describes the extended frame (see also *Chapter 4.6 - Extended CAN Protocol*). The first edition of ISO 11898-2, together with ISO 11898-1, replaces ISO 11898:1991, which has been technically revised.

---

[4] Source: http://www.can-cia.org

ISO 11898 consists of the following parts:

1. Data link layer and physical signaling
2. High-speed medium access unit
3. Low-speed, fault-tolerant, medium dependent interface
4. Time-triggered communication

The ISO 11898 standards are available as a download through ISO's website at http://www.iso.org. These documents provide an (almost complete) description of the CAN standard and even though the contents are sometimes rather sparse, it makes for an interesting reading, considering that good literature on CAN was hardly available up until now. The downside to the ISO documents, however, is that the download comes with a hefty price tag.

Chapter

2

MAIN CHARACTERISTICS

Everything that has to do with CAN is based on maximum reliability with the maximum possible performance in mind. After all, CAN was originally designed for automobiles, definitely a very demanding environment for microprocessors, not only in regards to required electrical robustness, but also due to high speed requirements for a serial communication system.

Many companies in the field of medical engineering chose CAN because they have to meet particularly strict safety requirements. Similar problems have been faced by manufacturers of other equipment with very high safety or reliability requirements, including robots, lifts and transportation systems.

The CAN properties can be summarized as:
- Multi-Master priority based bus access
- Non-destructive contention-based arbitration
- Multicast message transfer by message acceptance filtering
- Remote data request
- Configuration flexibility
- System-wide data consistency
- Error detection and error signaling
- Automatic retransmission of messages that lost arbitration
- Automatic retransmission of messages that were destroyed by errors
- Distinction between temporary errors and permanent failures of nodes
- Autonomous deactivation of defective nodes

2.1 FRAMES

In the language of the CAN standard, all messages are referred to as frames, such as data frames, remote frames, error frames, etc. Information sent to the CAN bus must be compliant to defined format frames of different but limited length.

Any node connected to the network may transmit a new frame as soon as the bus is idle. The consistency of a frame must be simultaneously accepted by all nodes in a CAN network.
CAN provides four different types of message frames:

> **Data Frame – Sends data**
  Data transfer from one sending node to one or numerous receiving nodes.
> **Remote Frame – Requests data**
  Any node may request data from another source node. A remote frame is consequently followed by a data frame containing the requested data.
> **Error Frame – Reports error condition**
  Any bus participant, sender or receiver, may signal an error condition at any time during a data or remote frame transmission.
> **Overload Frame – Reports node overload**
  A node can request a delay between two data or remote frames, meaning the overload frame can only occur between data or remote frame transmissions.

2.2 MULTI-MASTER BUS ACCESS

In order to assure a direct communication between nodes, therefore providing maximum speed combined with maximum reliability, CAN does not restrict itself to the popular client/master network configuration. In a typical CAN network all nodes have equal rights. Every node transmitting a data/remote frame will be the bus master during that transmission.

The actual bus access is managed through non-destructive bit-wise arbitration, which in turn provides very effective message collision avoidance in case that multiple nodes attempt to access the bus at the same time.

A possible bus access conflict is being resolved through contention-based arbitration using the message identifier. The CAN arbitration process assures in a very timely fashion that no information will be lost. The transmitter with the frame of highest priority (lowest message ID) will gain the bus access.

Frames that lost the arbitration and frames that were interrupted by error conditions will be retransmitted automatically as soon as the bus is idle again.

2.3 MESSAGE BROADCASTING

The broadcasting of messages is based on a producer-consumer principle. One node, when sending a message, will be the producer while all other nodes are the consumers. All nodes in a CAN network receive the same message at the same time.

In a multi-master network nodes may transmit data at any time. Each node "listens" to the network bus and will receive every transmitted message. The CAN Controller hardware in turn supports message-filtering, i.e. the receiving nodes will only react to data that is relevant to them.

Messages in CAN are not confirmed because that would unnecessarily increase the bus traffic. CAN assumes that all messages are compliant with the defined standard and if they are not, there will be a corresponding response by all nodes in the network (see also *Chapter 8.1 - Error Detection*). All receiving nodes check the consistency of the received frame and acknowledge the consistency. If the consistency is not acknowledged by any or all nodes in the network, the transmitter of the frame will post an error message to the bus.

If either one or more nodes are unable to decode a message, i.e. either detect an error in the message or are unable to read the message due to an internal malfunction, the entire bus will be notified of the error condition. Nodes that transmit faulty data or nodes that are constantly unable to receive a message correctly remove themselves from the bus (see *Chapter 8.3 - Fault Confinement*) and thus allow restoration of proper bus conditions.

The CAN standard also defines the request of a transmission from another node by means of a remote frame. The remote frame and the requested data frame use the same message identifier. They are, however, distinguished by the RTR bit (Remote Transmission Request) during the arbitration process (see also *Chapter 4 - Message Frame Architecture*).

2.4 MESSAGE PRIORITY

Per definition, CAN nodes are not concerned with information about the system configuration (e.g. node address, etc.), hence CAN does not support node IDs. Instead, receivers process messages by means of an acceptance filtering process, which decides whether the received message is relevant for node's application layer or not. There is no need for the receiver to know the transmitter of the information and vice versa.

CAN data transmissions are distinguished by a unique message identifier (11/29 bit), which also represents the message priority. A low message ID represents a high priority. A single CAN node may send or receive any number of messages, which contributes, yet again, to a maximum level of flexibility.

High priority messages will gain bus access within shortest time even when the bus load is high due to the number of lower priority messages.

Message transmissions are usually event-driven to reduce the bus load and that guarantees short latency times for real-time applications.

2.5 SHORT MESSAGES

CAN supports messages between 0 and 8 bytes of length. Initially this may seem to be a disadvantage compared to other technologies, but a short data length also assures short latency times for high priority messages. Additionally a limited data length contributes to the ability to withstand the strain of harsh electrical environments.

A message length of a maximum of 8 bytes is sufficient for data communications in cars, smaller machines such as household appliances and lower level automation. Higher-Layer protocols such as CANopen support segmented transmission of data of unlimited length that are more suitable for complex automation tasks such as motion control. However, CANopen still supports the limited 8 byte messages (Process Data Objects = PDO). These messages are usually assigned a high priority and, according to the CAN standard, they are able to interrupt the segmented transfer of low priority data (Service Data Object = SDO) after each completed data segment of 8 bytes. The low priority data transfer will resume right after the high priority message has been transmitted.

2.6 DATA RATE AND MESSAGE FREQUENCY

A maximum CAN baud rate of 1 MBit/sec may not sound much, but the combination of very short messages, the very effective collision avoidance, error detection and fault confinement capabilities, makes CAN much more suitable for real-time applications than, for instance, TCP/IP with its up to 100 MBit/sec transmission speed. After all, CAN was designed for real-time control, while TCP/IP was designed for data transfer where exact timing is not mandatory.

The maximum number of CAN messages per second is 8,771 (at 1 MBit/sec, 8 bytes per message), up to 17,543 at 1 MBit/sec and 1 byte per message (average bit stuffing applied, see also *Chapter 7.2 - Bit Stuffing*). This results in a data transfer between 17,543 and 70,168 data bytes per second.[5]

2.7 BUS ARBITRATION

Since a serial communication system such as CAN is based on a two-wire connection between nodes in the network, i.e. all nodes are sharing the same physical communication bus, a

---

[5] Net data transfer, without protocol overhead.

method of message/data collision avoidance is mandatory to assure a safe data transfer and to avoid delays resulting from the necessary restoration of proper bus conditions after the collision.

A collision may occur when two or more nodes in the network are attempting to access the bus at virtually the same time, which may result in unwelcome effects, such as bus access delays or even destruction or damage of messages.

CAN provides a non-destructive bus arbitration, i.e. no message gets lost. Higher priority messages will win the bus access, while low priority message wait until their time has come.

Based on a 1 MBit/sec baud rate and an 11 Bit message identifier, the arbitration process is finished after 12 microseconds.

2.8 ERROR DETECTION & FAULT CONFINEMENT

Rather than providing a message confirmation, which in turn would increase the bus load, CAN goes the more aggressive route of assuming that all messages must be consistent with the defined standard. Every diversion from this standard is detected and reported immediately, i.e. the error detection actually replaces the message confirmation. Naturally, confirmed messages would occur more often than actual error messages.

Each node in the network will receive each transmitted message. A message filter guarantees that the node knows when to ignore a message or to process it. However, each node in the network will check the transmitted message for compliance with the defined standard. All receiving nodes check the consistency of the received frame and acknowledge the consistency. If the consistency is not acknowledged by any or all nodes in the network, the transmitter of the frame will post an error frame to the bus.

The occurrence of an error frame may actually have two reasons. First, the transmitted data frame was really faulty or second, the data frame was correct, but one node erroneously reported an error due to a local reception problem.

It is important to distinguish between temporary errors or permanent failures of a node. CAN controllers address this problem by providing two different error counters, one for transmit errors and one for receive errors. If either counter exceeds a programmable limit, the node is considered faulty.

As part of the fault confinement, the CAN protocol allows the "removal" of a CAN node from the network, in case the node produces a constant stream of errors and therefore unnecessarily increases the bus load.

CAN also provides very short error recovery times of a maximum of 23 bit times. With a baud rate of 1 MBit/sec this translates into maximal 23 microseconds.

Chapter

3

BENEFITS OF USING CAN

Controller Area Network, like any field-bus system that is based on serial communication, will reduce wiring, which was originally considered only as an advantageous side effect. Distributed control, i.e. the use of a multi-processor system, will consequently result in increased performance and the vastly reduced costs of microcontroller chips in the market made the use of multiple processors in one system affordable. Other advantages are increased reliability and improved service and maintenance features.

Another major benefit of applying the CAN technology is apparent during the timely and therefore costly hardware and software development process. Two layers, the Physical Layer and the Data Link Layer, as defined in the ISO 11898 standard, are already implemented in silicon, either in the form of a stand-alone CAN controller or integrated in multi-function single-chip microcontrollers.

3.1 CAN Controller Firmware

As demonstrated in picture 3.1.1, the ISO/OSI Reference Model specifies 7 levels beginning with the physical connection up to the actual user application, i.e. the Application Layer.[6]

The standard CAN implementation bypasses the connection between the Data Link Layer and the Application Layer in order to save on valuable memory resources by minimizing the overhead and, as a result, gaining performance as needed for embedded solutions with limited resources.

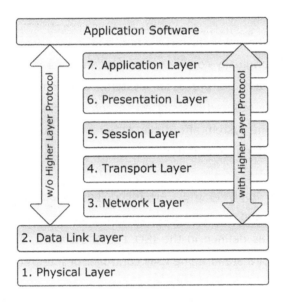

Picture 3.1.1: ISO/OSI 7 Layer Reference Model

Layers 3 through 6, i.e. all layers above the Data Link Layer, require additional software resources, which are provided by higher layer protocols such as CANopen, DeviceNet and J1939 (see *Chapter 3.5 - Higher Layer Protocols*).

---

[6] For more information on the OSI Reference Model refer to:
CertificationZone.com OSI Reference Model Pocket Guide
by Howard C. Berkowitz - ISBN: 1890911143

Hear Ye! Hear Ye!

Whenever you attempt to add software functions between the CAN Data Link Layer and the Application Layer, you will be adding functionalities that are already covered by off-the-shelf available higher layer protocols such as CANopen and DeviceNet.

The **Application Layer** is the layer that actually interacts with the operating system or application of the CAN device.

The **Data Link Layer** connects the actual data to the protocol in terms of sending, receiving and validating data. Under CAN it represents the data exchange including error detection/recovery and fault confinement, transmission acknowledgements, etc., and all the ingenious features as previously described in *Chapter 2 - Main Characteristics*.

The **Physical Layer** represents the actual hardware, i.e. the physical connection between nodes in a network and the electrical signal characteristics such as voltage levels and timing.

The software development engineer will benefit from the fact that under CAN the two lowest layers, the Physical Layer and Data Link Layer, are already integrated into silicon. This reduces the software development process by concentrating solely on the coding of the actual application software.

Most CAN chip manufacturers and vendors, who are in the CAN business, do provide source code (e.g. for LINUX) and libraries (e.g. Windows APIs) for all function calls that represent the connection between the Data Link Layer and the Application Layer.

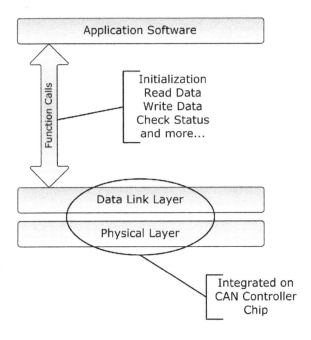

Picture 3.1.2: CAN Controller Chip in the 7-Layer Model

The nature of the necessary function calls is identical to those needed for the access of any hardware device (drivers):

> Initialization

> Read Data

> Write Date

> Check Status

Naturally, this is just a very basic list of function calls. Most code libraries provide extended functionality like the determination of the bus load, and more.

3.2 LOW COST IMPLEMENTATION

Most major semiconductor manufacturers, including Motorola, Philips, Intel, Infineon, among others, sell CAN chips, and the fact that millions of them are used in automobiles guarantees low chip prices.

As a matter of fact, implementing CAN into a new application can be accomplished with less hardware costs and less development time than, for instance, RS232/485 or TCP/IP.

CAN software libraries, even including CANopen or DeviceNet protocol stacks, require a significant lower memory footprint and far less CPU performance than any TCP/IP implementation.

3.3 SPEED, RELIABILITY, ERROR-RESISTANCE

CAN provides the ability to function in difficult electrical environments, a high degree of real time capability and ease of use. The real time capabilities are supported by extremely short arbitration times in the range of microseconds, limited data length and extremely short error recovery times, again, in the range of microseconds.

The reliability and error resistance of CAN has been calculated in a mathematical model. Here is an example using the following parameters and conditions:

➢ 1 Bit error every 0.7 sec
➢ Baud rate of 500 kBit/sec
➢ Operation of 8 hours/day and 365 days/year

According to the mathematical model the *Residual Error Probability* will be **1 undetected error in 1000 years**.[7]

3.4 WORLDWIDE ACCEPTANCE

The CAN technology is supported by many suppliers and manufacturers all over the world who provide CAN controllers, CAN interface boards, CAN analyzing software tools and higher layer protocols.

---

[7] Source: CAN-in-Automation

As was emphasized previously, many major semiconductor manufacturers, including Motorola, Philips, Intel, Infineon, among, sell CAN chips, and the fact that millions of them are used in automobiles guarantees low chip prices and long-term availability.

The use of CAN in most of European passenger cars and the decision by truck and off-road vehicle manufacturers for CAN led to the availability of CAN chips since 1987.

Other high volume markets, like domestic appliances and industrial control, also increase the CAN sales figures and guarantee the availability for the future.

3.5 HIGHER LAYER PROTOCOLS

Even though extremely effective in automobiles and small applications, CAN alone is not suitable for machine automation, since its communication between devices is limited to only 8 bytes. As a consequence, higher layer protocols such as CANopen for machine control, DeviceNet for factory automation and J1939 for vehicles were designed to provide a real networking technology that support messages of unlimited length and allow a master/slave configuration.

In order to explain higher layer protocols we must refer again to the ISO/OSI Reference Model as shown in picture 3.5.1.[8]

---

[8] For more information on the OSI Reference Model refer to:
CertificationZone.com OSI Reference Model Pocket Guide
by Howard C. Berkowitz - ISBN: 1890911143

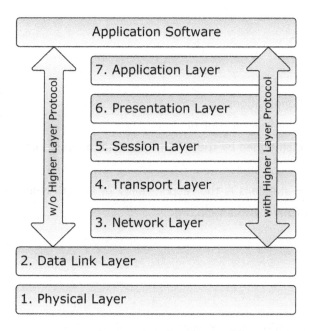

Picture 3.5.1: ISO/OSI 7 Layer Reference Model

The standard CAN implementation bypasses the connection between the Data Link Layer and the Application Layer. The layers above the Data Link Layer are covered by additional software, which represents per definition a higher layer protocol.

To emphasize it again, whenever you attempt to add software functions between the CAN Data Link Layer and the Application Layer, you will be adding functionalities that are already covered by off-the-shelf available higher layer protocols such as CANopen and DeviceNet.

To put it in a nut shell, higher layer protocols are necessary, because

> ➤ They enable data transport of more than 8 bytes per message
> ➤ Embedded Systems may require an appropriate communication model based on Master/Slave configuration
> ➤ They provide Network Management (Network Start-Up, Node Monitoring, Node Synchronization, etc.)

CANopen

Is suited for embedded applications

Was originally designed for motion control

Was developed and is maintained by the CAN-in-Automation User Group

Like CAN, the CANopen standard is the responsibility of CiA (CAN-in-Automation). For further information, refer to http://www.can-cia.org.

DeviceNet

- ➢ Is suited for industrial applications (floor automation)
- ➢ Was developed by Allen Bradley/Rockwell
- ➢ Is maintained by Open DeviceNet Vendor Association (ODVA)

The DeviceNet Specification, consisting of two volumes: Volume One - Common Industrial Protocol (CIP) and Volume Three- DeviceNet Adaptation of CIP, is available only for ODVA (Open DeviceNet Vendor Association) members.

For further information, refer to http://www.odva.org.

SAE J1939

- ➢ Defines communication for vehicle networks (trucks, buses, agricultural equipment, etc.)
- ➢ Is a standard developed by the Society of Automotive Engineers (SAE)

The SAE J1939 Standards Collection can be found exclusively on the Web at http://www.sae.org[9].

The Society of Automotive Engineers (SAE) Truck and Bus Control and Communications Subcommittee has developed a family of standards concerning the design and use of devices that transmit electronic signals and control information among vehicle components. SAE J1939 and its companion documents have quickly become the accepted industry standard and the Controller Area Network (CAN) of choice for off-highway machines in applications such as construction, material handling, and forestry machines.

---

[9] For further information on SAE J1939 refer to *A Comprehensible Guide to J1939* by the same author (http://www.copperhillmedia.com/J1939Book.html).

Chapter

4

MESSAGE FRAME ARCHITECTURE

After a lengthy, but necessary introduction it is time to explain the technical features of CAN in detail. The following chapter explains the CAN message frames by bit and bytes. Further chapters will address the mechanism of message broadcasting, the bus arbitration and the actual physical layer.

In the language of the CAN standard, all messages are referred to as frames; there are data frames, remote frames, error frames and overload frames. Information sent to the CAN bus must be compliant to defined frame formats of different but limited length.

CAN provides four different types of message frames:

- ➢ **Data Frame – Sends data**
  Data transfer from one sending node to one or numerous receiving nodes.

- ➢ **Remote Frame – Requests data**[10]
  Any node may request data from one source node. A remote frame is consequently followed by a data frame containing the requested data.

---

[10] The use of Remote Frames is not recommended (See also chapter *4.4.1 Remote Frames on Recall*)

➢ **Error Frame – Reports error condition**

Any bus participant, sender or receiver, may signal an error condition at any time during a data or remote frame transmission.

➢ **Overload Frame – Reports node overload**[11]

A node can request a delay between two data or remote frames, meaning that the overload frame can only occur between data or remote frame transmissions.

The distance between consecutive frames is a minimum of 3 bit times (Interframe Space, see also *Chapter 4.5 - Message Frame Format*).

An 11 bit identifier (standard format) allows a total of 2^{11} (= 2048) different messages. A 29 bit identifier (extended format) allows a total of 2^{29} (= 536+ million) messages (see also *Chapter 4.6 - Extended CAN Protocol*).

Both, Data Frame and Remote Frame, are very similar. Basically, the Remote Frame is a Data Frame without the Data Field. Error frames and overload frames have a different format, which will be explained in more detail in a later chapter. In order to explain the various frames and their differences, it is necessary to have a first look into the CAN serial bus bit by bit.

4.1 DOMINANT AND RECESSIVE BUS LEVEL

However, before going into the details of each bit in a CAN frame it is helpful to have a brief look ahead into the physical layer (For more details refer to *Chapter 9 - Physical Layer*) in order to understand the nature of, for instance, the SOF (Start of Frame) bit, the RTR (Remote Transmission Request) bit and, in a later chapter, the bus arbitration.

As its name clearly implies, the SOF bit signals the beginning of a message frame. The RTR bit separates the data from the remote frame. Understanding the dominant and recessive level on the CAN bus makes it easier to understand the differentiation between data and remote frame.

---

[11] Considering today's technologies an overload frames should not occur. As a matter of fact, some modern CAN controllers do not support the Overload Frame anymore.

The physical CAN bus uses a differential voltage between two wires, CAN_H and CAN_L. A CAN controller with its TTL output uses an additional line driver (transceiver) to provide the standard CAN level (see Chapter 9 - Physical Layer). The following chapters on the CAN frame architecture and bus arbitration refer to the TTL output of the CAN controller.[12]

Hear Ye! Hear Ye!

The dominant level (TTL = 0V) always overrides a recessive level (TTL = 5V), which is important especially during bus arbitration.

As demonstrated in picture 4.1.1 the CAN bus level will be dominant in case any number of nodes in the network output a dominant level. The CAN bus level will only be recessive when all nodes in the network output a recessive level.

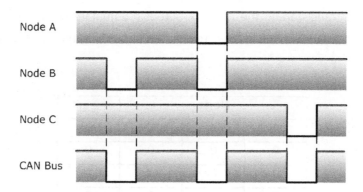

Picture 4.1.1: CAN Node Output and Bus Level

An equivalent from some electronics basics will explain the relationship between node output and the resulting bus level as shown in picture 4.1.2.

---

[12] Most works on Controller Area Network fail to mention this little, but nevertheless very important fact before they refer to CAN frames, which may lead to the incorrect perception that CAN_L is the dominant level and CAN_H is the recessive bus level.

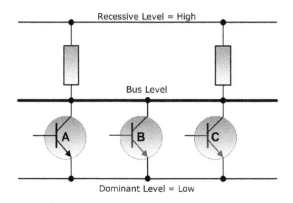

Picture 4.1.2: Open Collector Principle on a CAN bus

This example uses three nodes in a CAN network, in this case represented by three transistors in open-collector ("Wired And") configuration. The bus level will be at low level (dominant) in case any number of transistors in the network output a dominant level. The bus level will only be at high level (recessive) when all transistors in the network output a recessive level.

Node			
A	**B**	**C**	**Bus**
0	0	0	0
0	0	1	0
0	1	0	0
0	1	1	0
1	0	0	0
1	0	1	0
1	1	0	0
1	1	1	1

Table 4.1.1: Wired And

The following picture demonstrates the transition from an idle CAN bus to an SOF (Start of Frame), meaning the initiation of a new message transfer.

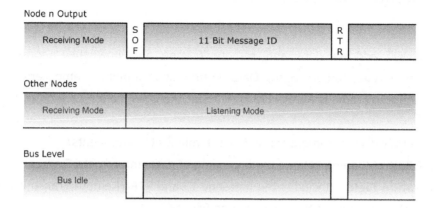

Picture 4.1.3: Bus Level Example

Picture 4.1.3 shows the output signal of a CAN node in comparison with the actual bus level.

While the bus is idle, i.e. no node attempts a transmission, the bus will remain on the recessive level.

When one or more nodes attempt to start a transmission they will output the SOF (Start of Frame) bit to the bus. An active SOF bit is per definition at dominant level; therefore an active SOF bit will set the bus to the dominant level.

The bus arbitration mechanism will decide which of the nodes requesting bus access will succeed (refer to *Chapter 6 - Bus Arbitration*).

The example as shown in picture 4.1.3 demonstrates the transmission of a data frame, which is indicated by a dominant RTR (Remote Transmission Request). A recessive RTR bit would indicate the presence of a remote frame, a frame requesting data from another node.

In theory the data frame in picture 4.1.3 could be the response to a remote frame. The remote frame and the requested data frame use the same message identifier (see also *Chapter 4.4 - Remote Frame*). The RTR bit, like the message ID, is part of the arbitration field.

A dominant RTR (Remote Transmission Request) bit, indicating a Data Frame, will override a recessive RTR bit (indicating a Remote Frame). As a result, in case that a Remote and Data Frame with the same message ID try to access the bus, the Data Frame will have higher priority than the Remote Frame requesting the data.

4.2 Data and Remote Frames

The following will address data and remote frames and how they, consequently, are distinguished from each other. Both, Data Frame and Remote Frame, are very similar. Basically, the Remote Frame is a Data Frame without the Data Field.

Per definition a CAN data or remote frame has the following components:

 - ➢ **SOF** (Start of Frame) - Marks the beginning of data and remote Frames
 - ➢ **Arbitration Field** – Includes the message ID and RTR (Remote Transmission Request) bit, which distinguishes data and remote frames
 - ➢ **Control Field** – Used to determine data size and message ID length
 - ➢ **Data Field** – The actual data (Applies only to a data frame, not a remote frame)
 - ➢ **CRC Field** - Checksum
 - ➢ **EOF** (End of Frame) – Marks the end of data and remote frames

Picture 4.2.1: CAN Data Frame Architecture

Picture 4.2.2 shows the CAN frame in more detail.

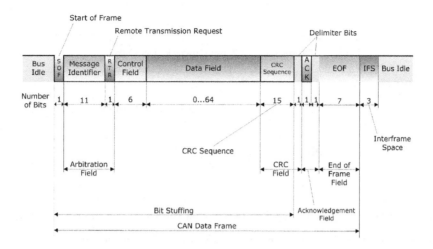

Picture 4.2.2: Detailed CAN Data Frame Architecture

Each CAN message starts with a "Start of Frame" bit (SOF), followed by the message identifier and the "Remote Transmission Request" bit (RTR). This particular bit, the RTR bit, is now the focus in explaining the difference between a Data Frame and a Remote Frame, which are both very similar. A more detailed explanation of the CAN message frame will follow in *Chapter 4.5 - Message Frame Format*.

4.3 DATA FRAME

A Data Frame broadcasts a message, the actual data, to the CAN bus, either due to change of an event (for example, the change of an input signal, a timer event, etc.) or as a response to a message request. The data frame, identified by a unique message ID, may be accepted by any number of nodes in the network according to the individual application needs, but can only be transmitted by the (one and only) node associated with the data message.

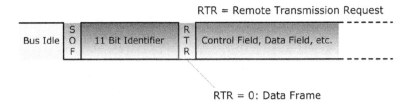

Picture 4.3.1: RTR in a Data Frame

Between the Start of Frame (SOF) bit and the end of the message identifier, both frames, Data Frames and Remote Frames, are absolutely identical. A Data Frame is detected by a low (dominant) RTR (Remote Transmission Request) bit. Each receiving node in a CAN network, when detecting a low RTR bit, will now know that the received message is a Data Frame. In fact the RTR bit is part of the arbitration portion of a message frame.

Hear Ye! Hear Ye!

The remote frame and the requested data frame use the same message identifier (see also Chapter 4.4 - Remote Frame). Both frames are distinguished by the RTR (Remote Transmission Request) bit, which is part of the arbitration field. In case a data frame and a remote frame using the same message ID try to access the bus simultaneously, the data frame will gain the bus access over the remote frame, since it uses a dominant RTR bit.

Picture 4.3.2: Data Frame Architecture

Picture 4.3.2 shows the complete Data Frame. Since the Data Frame and the Remote Frame are built very similar, a detailed description of both frames' building stones is provided in a dedicated section, *Chapter 4.5 - Message Frame Format.*

4.4 REMOTE FRAME

A Remote Frame requests the transmission of a message by another node. The requested data frame, identified by a unique message ID, may be accepted by any number of nodes in the network according to the individual application needs, but can only be sent by <u>one</u> node associated with the requested message.

The remote frame and the requested data frame use the same message identifier. Both frames are distinguished by the RTR (Remote Transmission Request) bit, which is part of the arbitration field. In case a data frame and a remote frame using the same message ID try to access the bus simultaneously, the data frame will gain the bus access over the remote frame, since it uses a dominant RTR bit.

Remote frames can only be transmitted with a DLC (Data Length Code) identical to the DLC of the corresponding data frame. Due to a limitation of a contention-based arbitration, simultaneous transmission of remote frames with different DLCs will lead to irresolvable collisions. See also Chapter 4.5 - Message Frame Format.

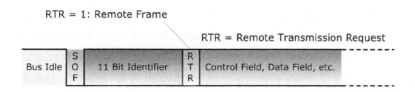

Picture 4.4.1: RTR in a Remote Frame

Between the Start of Frame (SOF) bit and the end of the message identifier, both frames, Data Frames and Remote Frames, are absolutely identical. A Remote Frame is detected by a high (recessive) RTR bit (Remote Transmission Request). Each receiving node in a CAN network, when detecting a high RTR bit, will now know that the received message is a Remote Frame. In fact the RTR bit is part of the arbitration portion of a message frame.

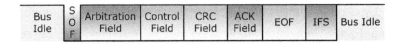

Picture 4.4.2: Remote Frame Architecture

Picture 4.4.2 shows the complete Remote Frame. Since the Data Frame and the Remote Frame are built very similar, a detailed description of both frames' building components is provided in the following *Chapter 4.5 Message Frame Format*.

The data request cycle in a CAN network will involve the sending of two messages, the actual message request (remote frame), followed by the requested data (data frame). For further details please refer also to Chapter 5 - Message Broadcasting.

4.4.1 REMOTE FRAME ON RECALL

Experience over the years has uncovered some oddities in the CAN protocol - which are naturally not covered by any official document - and one of them has lead to the call to avoid CAN remote frames. In August of 2005 CAN-in-Automation (CiA) released (but not promoted) their application note 802 - "CAN remote frame - Avoiding of usage". The document can be requested through the 'Contac Us' section on their web site (http://www.can-cia.org).

As a reminder, data frame and remote frame are very similar. Basically, the remote frame is a data frame without the data field (which would be located between the Control Field and the CRC Filed). Data frame and remote frame are distinguished by the RTR bit in the arbitration field (Data frame: RTR=0, Remote Frame: RTR=1).

One source of the problem with the remote frame is based in the way the Control Field, especially the data length code, is being transmitted:

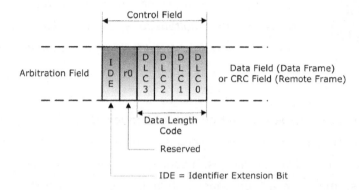

Picture 4.4.1: Control Field

For further detailed information on the Control Field and the Data Length Code, please refer also to the next chapter *4.5 Message Frame Format*.

The actual problem lies in protocol-incompatibilities between CAN controllers of different manufacturers and how they handle the Remote Frame, which consequently will result in bus collisions.[13]

A bus collision may occur under the following conditions:
- Two or more CAN nodes in a network request the same message at the same time or remote frame and requested data frame access the bus at the same time (latter condition is not mentioned in the CiA application note).
- The data length codes differ between the nodes.

---

[13] As was pointed out throughout this document, the official description of the CAN protocol leaves ample room for interpretation. In this particular case it did lead to different results between chip designers.

 *The remote frame and the requested data frame use the same message identifier. Both frames are distinguished by the RTR (Remote Transmission Request) bit, which is part of the arbitration field. In case a data frame and a remote frame using the same message ID try to access the bus simultaneously, the data frame will gain the bus access over the remote frame, since it uses a dominant RTR bit.*

Remote frames can only be transmitted with a data length code (DLC) identical to the DLC of the corresponding data frame. Simultaneous transmission of remote frames with different DLC's will lead to irresolvable collisions, meaning the CAN bit monitoring feature will detect an error. That also means in all consequence that the requesting node **must** know the correct DLC.

What happens next is the same as when two frames with the same message ID try to access the bus. This result of this scenario has so far not been documented in any official literature. The official statement is that such scenarios are not allowed and will lead to unpredictable results. However, as CiA application note 802 explains, there are quite some discrepancies between the numerous CAN controllers available in the market and how they handle remote frames. It appears that collisions can occur with such probability that the use of remote frames is not recommended at all.

CAN Remote Frames under CANopen

The use of remote frames under CANopen is restricted per design, however, the problem remains. The wording in the CiA application note 802 almost suggests that the problem has been taken care of, but that is only true when certain rules are being followed:

- **Network Management:** Use heartbeat rather than node-guarding functions, since this does not involve remote frames.

- **Polling of Process Data Objects (PDOs):** Use a scheduling function for the transmission of PDOs; however, do not use remote frames for the scheduling. CANopen provides two modes, centralized and decentralized scheduling of PDOs (please refer to the CANopen standard DS-301 and DSP-302).

4.5 MESSAGE FRAME FORMAT

In this section the exact structure of both, data and remote message frame, will be explained bit by bit.

Per definition a CAN data or remote frame has the following components:

> **SOF** (Start of Frame) - Marks the beginning of data and remote Frames
>
> **Arbitration Field** – Includes the message ID and RTR (Remote Transmission Request) bit, which distinguishes data and remote frames
>
> **Control Field** – Used to determine data size and message ID length
>
> **Data Field** – The actual data (Applies only to a data frame, not a remote frame)
>
> **CRC Field** - Checksum
>
> **ACK Field** – Acknowledgement of checksum check
>
> **EOF** (End of Frame) – Marks the end of data and remote frames
>
> **IFS** – Interframe Space

Both, Data Frame and Remote Frame, are very similar. Basically, the Remote Frame is a Data Frame without the Data Field.

• **Data Frame**

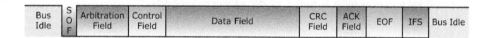

Picture 4.5.1: Data Frame Architecture

• **Remote Frame**

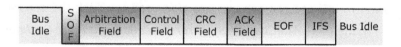

Picture 4.5.2: Remote Frame Architecture

The following picture (4.5.3) shows the bit stream of a data frame in detail.

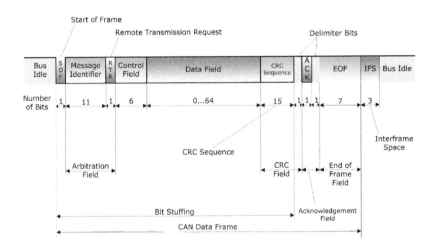

Picture 4.5.3: Detailed Data/Remote Frame Architecture

The entire frame as shown in picture 4.5.3 has a length between 47 and 111 bits, depending on the length of data field, which can be between 0 and 8 bytes (0 and 64 bits).

At a baud rate of 1 MBit/sec this translates into a transmission time between 47 (remote frame) and 111 (data frame with 8 bytes of data) microseconds.[14]

The following components of a CAN data or remote frame are considered static fields, since their data level is static (recessive):[15]

> ➤ CRC Delimiter
> ➤ ACK Delimiter
> ➤ End of Frame Field
> ➤ Intermission FieldThese components are also used to check the consistency of a data
> or remote frame (see also *Chapter 8 - Error Detection and Fault Confinement*).

---

[14] The information on frame length and the derived transmission times do not include any stuffing bits (See also *Chapter 7.2 - Bit Stuffing*). In all consequence, the number of average bit stuffing needs to be applied. For more detailed information on frame length and transmission time refer to *Chapter 4.10 - Frame Length and Transmission Times*.
[15] The ISO 11898-1 and the Bosch/CiA standard refer to the static fields in various chapters, but omit a precise definition.

Each CAN message frame, regardless of the message ID length, will be terminated by a sequence of 11 recessive bits: The ACK Delimiter bit in the Acknowledgement Field (1 bit), the End of Frame Field (7 bits) and the Intermission Field (3 bits).

The individual frame elements are:

> **SOF (1 Bit)**
>
> The dominant Start of Frame (SOF) bit represents the start of a Data/Remote Frame and, in all consequence, also starts the arbitration sequence (the arbitration field follows right after the SOF bit). A CAN node, before attempting to access the bus, must wait until the bus is idle. An idle bus is detected by a sequence of 11 recessive bits, i.e. the sequence of ACK Delimiter bit in the Acknowledgement Field (1 bit), the End of Frame Field (7 bits) and the Intermission Field (3 bits).

The falling (leading) edge of the SOF bit (transition from recessive to dominant level), sent by the first node that attempts to access the bus, also serves as a mechanism to synchronize all CAN bus nodes.

> **Arbitration Field (12 or 32 Bit)**

The arbitration field contains of two components:

- 11/29 Bit Message Identifier, first Bit is MSB. As will be explained later, the CAN message ID can be 11 or 29 bits long.
- RTR (Remote Transmission Request) indicates either the transmission of a Data Frame (RTR = 0) or a Remote-Request Frame (RTR = 1).

A low message ID number represents a high message priority.
A Data Frame has higher priority than a Remote Frame.

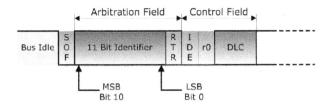

Picture 4.5.4: Arbitration Field with 11-Bit Identifier

The total length of the arbitration field is 12 bits when an 11 bit message identifier is used (see picture 4.5.4).

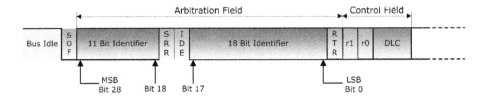

Picture 4.5.5: Arbitration Field with 29-Bit Identifier

As shown in picture 4.5.5, the total length of the arbitration field will be 32 bit with a 29 bit identifier (see also *Chapter 4.6 - Extended CAN Protocol*).

An 11 bit identifier (standard format) allows a total of 2^{11} (= 2048) different messages. A 29 bit identifier (extended format) allows a total of 2^{29} (= 536+ million) messages.

The IDE (Identifier Extension) bit belongs to:

> ➤ The **Control Field** of the standard format (11 bit message identifier)
> ➤ The **Arbitration Field** of the extended format (29 bit message identifier)

➢ **Control Field (6 Bits)**

The 4 LSB bits of the Control Field specify the length of the data block (DLC = Data Length Code), the MSB bit (IDE = Identifier Extension) indicates either standard 11-Bit format (Bit = 0) or 29-Bit extended format (Bit = 1).

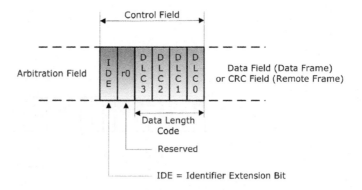

Picture 4.5.6: Control Field

As will be explained in the following chapter, the CAN message ID can be 11 or 29 bits long. The IDE bit became active with the release of the CAN 2.0B standard (i.e. the extension of the message identifier from 11 to 29 bits). The previous standard CAN 2.0A referred to bits r0 and r1 (instead of IDE), which were, at the time, reserved for future purposes. Both bits, r0 and r1, were always sent as dominant (zero), which, according to standard CAN 2.0B, indicates an 11 bit identifier per default.

The Data Length Code (DLC) is usually set to a value between 0 and 8 indicating a data field length between 0 and 8 bytes. A value greater than 8 is permissible for application specific purposes. In this case the sending node must send 8 data bytes, while the receiving nodes are expecting 8 bytes.

Remote frames can only be transmitted with a DLC (Data Length Code) identical to the DLC of the corresponding data frame. Due to a limitation of a contention-based arbitration simultaneous transmission of remote frames with different DLCs will lead to irresolvable collisions.

> **Data Field**

Maximum 8 bytes, first Bit is MSB.

> **CRC Field (16 Bits)**

The CRC (Cyclical Recovery Checking) Field contains of the CRC Sequence and a CRC Delimiter Bit.

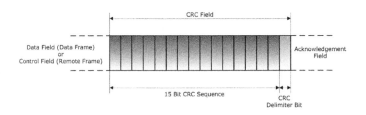

Picture 4.5.7: CRC Field

The 15 bit **CRC Segment** contains the frame check sequence spanning from SOF (Start of Frame), through the arbitration field, control field and data field. Stuffing Bits are not included (see also *Chapter 7.2 - Bit Stuffing*).

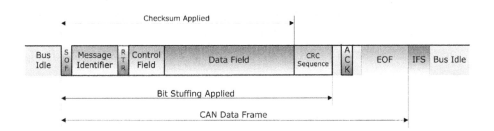

Picture 4.5.8: Range of Checksum Application

 *The frame check sequence is derived from a CRC (BCH = Bose-Chaudhuri-Hocquenghem code) best suited for frame lengths of less than 127 bits.*

The **CRC Delimiter Bit** (always recessive, i.e. 1), following right behind the CRC Segment, allows for CRC processing time.

➤ **Acknowledgement Field (2 Bits)**

The Acknowledgement Field contains of a 1 bit Acknowledgement Slot plus the ACK Delimiter Bit (which is always recessive).

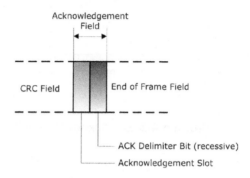

Picture 4.5.9: Acknowledgement Field

Unlike other serial communications, such as RS232, the acknowledgement field does not serve as a signal for the successful or unsuccessful reception of a message by a receiving node (consider that there may be numerous receiving nodes in a CAN network). The acknowledgement field serves as a confirmation of a successful CRC (checksum) check by the receiving nodes in the network.

During the ACK slot, the message transmitting node switches to receive mode by sending a recessive signal to the bus. At the same time all other nodes in the network accomplish their individual CRC (checksum) check (according to the CAN standard all nodes must determine the checksum in the same standardized way) and output a dominant signal to the bus if the check was successful.

The message transmitting node monitors the bus and expects a dominant level during the ACK slot. This will be the case when either one of the receiving CAN nodes outputs a dominant level.

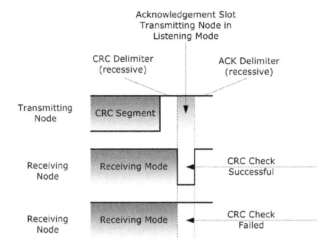

Picture 4.5.10: Acknowledgement Function

In the case that all nodes in the network determine a checksum error, meaning the sending node monitors a recessive level in the ACK slot, it is clear that the sending node calculated a wrong checksum. The error is therefore local at the sending node.

Any receiving node detecting a checksum error will post an error frame to the bus, i.e. right after the completed acknowledgement field. With this scenario it is possible to determine whether or not the actual malfunction is with that particular receiving node.

It is possible that the ACK slot remains dominant, while at the same time an error is reported by only one receiving node, meaning this single node will send out an error frame. The error is therefore local at that particular receiving node.

The CAN standard allows the so-called "self-retirement" (or self-removal) of nodes from the network due to an excessive number of transmit or receive errors (see also *Chapter 8 - Error Detection and Fault Confinement*).

The ACK Delimiter Bit is always recessive. This is necessary in order to distinguish a successful acknowledgement from an occurring error frame. An error frame starts with at least 6 successive dominant bits, meaning the first bit of an error frame will override the ACK Delimiter Bit (see also *Chapter 4.7 - Error Frame*).

> ➢ **End-of-Frame Field (7 bits, recessive)**

Each data or remote frame is terminated by a bit sequence of 7 recessive bits.

 *Each CAN message frame, regardless of the message ID length, will be terminated by a sequence of 11 recessive bits: The ACK Delimiter bit in the Acknowledgement Field (1 bit), the End of Frame Field (7 bits) and the Intermission Field (3 bits).*

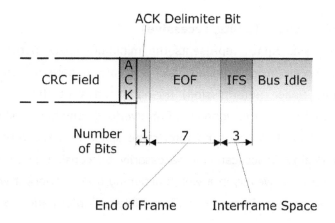

Picture 4.5.11: End-of-Frame Field

This last statement is actually only true, unless an Overload Frame occurs (see also *Chapter 4.8 - Overload Frame*).

More specifically: With the combination of the EOF Field and the preceding recessive ACK Delimiter Bit each message (data and remote) frame is terminated by 8 recessive bits plus, unless an overload frame occurs, the 3 recessive bits of the Intermission Field.

As shown in the following picture, the up to 11 recessive bits at the end of a message frame are not subject to bit stuffing error detection, since the bit stuffing applies only between the SOF (Start Of Frame) bit and (including) the CRC Sequence (see also *Chapter 7.2 - Bit Stuffing*).

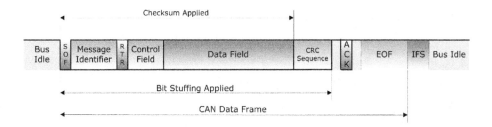

Picture 4.5.12: Bit Stuffing Range

> **Interframe Space (3 bits, recessive)**

The Interframe Space represents the minimum space between frames of any type (data, remote, error, overload) and a following data or remote frame. During the Interframe Space (intermission) no node can start the transmission of a data or remote frame. Only the signaling of an overload condition is allowed (see *Chapter 4.8 - Overload Frame*). There is no Interframe space between error and overload frames. The Interframe Space can not necessarily be considered to be a part of a data or remote frame, however, in a well functioning CAN network it will always follow behind a data or remote frame. For more detailed information see also *Chapter 4.9 - Interframe Space*.

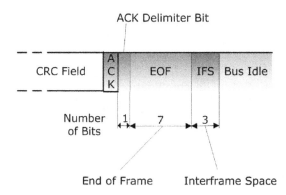

Picture 4.5.13: Interframe Space

4.6 EXTENDED CAN PROTOCOL

The standard CAN message frame uses an 11-bit message identifier (CAN 2.0A), which is sufficient for the use in regular automobiles and any industrial application, however, not necessarily for off-road vehicles.

The Society of Automotive Engineers (SAE) Truck and Bus Control and Communications Subcommittee had developed a family of standards concerning the design and use of devices that transmit electronic signals and control information among vehicle components. As a result, the higher layer protocol SAE J1939, based on CAN, was born, which was required to provide some backward-compatible functionality to older RS-232-based communication protocols (J1708/J1587).

In order to serve these demands, the CAN standard needed to be enhanced to support a 29 bit message identifier. The ISO 11898 amendment for an extended frame format (CAN 2.0B) was introduced in 1995.

The 29 bit message identifier consists of the regular 11 bit base identifier and an 18 bit identifier extension. The distinction between CAN base frame format and CAN extended frame format is accomplished by using the IDE bit inside the Control Field (See picture 4.6.2). A low (dominant) IDE bit indicates an 11 bit message identifier; a high (recessive) IDE bit indicates a 29 bit identifier.

An 11 bit identifier (standard format) allows a total of 2^{11} (= 2048) different messages. A 29 bit identifier (extended format) allows a total of 2^{29} (= 536+ million) messages.

Hear Ye! Hear Ye!

Both formats, Standard (11 bit message ID) and Extended (29 bit message ID), may co-exist on the same CAN bus. During bus arbitration the standard 11 bit message ID frame will always have higher priority than the extended 29 bit message ID frame with identical 11 bit base identifier and thus gain bus access.

 *The Extended Format has some trade-offs: The bus latency time is longer (minimum 20 bit-times), messages in extended format require more bandwidth (about 20 %), and the error detection performance is reduced (because the chosen polynomial for the 15-bit CRC is optimized for frame length up to 112 bits).*

Picture 4.6.1 shows the Control Field of a CAN data or remote frame according to the original CAN standard 2.0A:

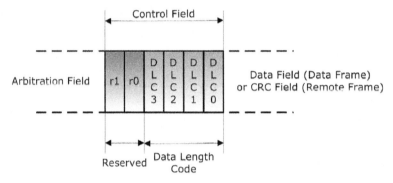

Picture 4.6.1: Control Field according to CAN 2.0A

Both bits, r1 and r0, were reserved for future use and were kept at a low (dominant) level.

The Control Field was "re-designed" (CAN 2.0B) as shown in picture 4.6.2 in order to support co-existence of 11 and 29 bit identifiers on the same CAN bus.

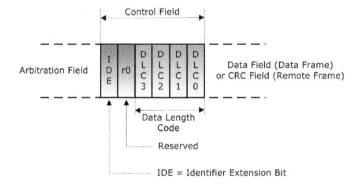

Picture 4.6.2: Control Field according to CAN 2.0B

A low (dominant) IDE bit indicates an 11 bit message identifier, a high (recessive) IDE bit indicates a 29 bit identifier.

• **Standard Format: 11 Bit message identifier**

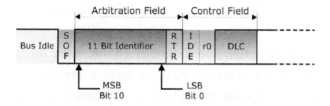

Picture 4.6.3: 11-Bit Message Identifer

A low (dominant) IDE bit indicates an 11 bit message identifier.

• **Extended Format: 29 Bit message identifier**

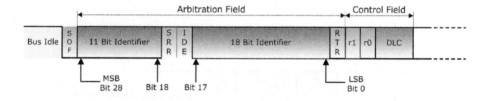

Picture 4.6.4: 29-Bit Message Identifier

A high (recessive) IDE bit indicates a 29 bit identifier.

 *The IDE (Identifier Extension) bit belongs to:*
> ➤ *The **Control Field** of the Standard Format*
> ➤ *The **Arbitration Field** of the Extended Format*

The 29 bit message identifier consists of the regular 11 bit base identifier and an 18 bit identifier extension. Between the SOF (Start of Frame) bit and the end of the 11 bit (base) message identifier, both frame formats, Standard and Extended, are identical.

Following the 11 bit base identifier, the Extended Format uses an (always recessive) SRR (Substitute Remote Request) bit, which, as its name implies, replaces the regular RTR (Remote Transmission Request). The following IDE (Identifier Extension) bit is also kept at a recessive level.

With the use of a recessive SRR plus a recessive IDE bit it is guaranteed that standard message frames (11 bit identifier) will always have higher priority than extended message frames (29 bit identifier) with identical 11 bit base identifier (see also *Chapter 6 - Bus Arbitration*).

The Control Field of an extended message frame, following the 18 bit extended identifier plus RTR bit, has the format of the original CAN 2.0A standard.

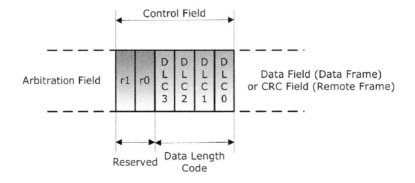

Picture 4.6.5: Control Field following the 18-Bit extended identifier

Bits r1 and r0 are reserved for future use and are always kept at a dominant level.

4.7 ERROR FRAME

An error frame initiates the termination of a faulty data or remote frame. This is actually accomplished through an intended violation of the CAN standard.

For purposes of synchronizing the time bases between all nodes in a network (see *Chapter 7 - Data Transfer Synchronization*) the CAN standard allows only 5 consecutive bits of the same polarity between the SOF bit and (including) the CRC Field of a message frame; every bit stream of more than 5 bits of the same polarity, dominant or recessive, is considered an error condition. As a matter of fact, CAN uses this rule to send an error frame, which contains of (minimum) 6 consecutive dominant bits. Each node in the network will recognize the violation of the standard and initiate the appropriate response.

In order to transmit or receive data that contains more than 5 bits of the same polarity the CAN standard requires the insertion (by the sending node) and filtering (by the receiving) of a complimentary bit of reversed polarity, the so-called Stuff Bit (see also *Chapter 7.2 - Bit Stuffing*).

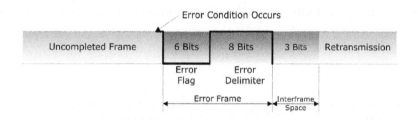

Picture 4.7.1: Basic Error Frame Architecture

An error frame signals the detection of an error condition by a receiving or transmitting node (see also *Chapter 8 - Error Detection and Fault Confinement*). The intended violation of the CAN standard (i.e. the sending of 6 dominant bits) guarantees the destruction of a faulty data or remote frame.

As shown in picture 4.7.1 the error frame consists of the 6 bit error flag and an 8 bit error delimiter. However, it demonstrates only the basic error frame according to the CAN standard.

As previously mentioned, a sequence of more than 5 consecutive bits of the same polarity between the SOF bit and (including) the CRC Field is considered an error condition. An error frame, posted by any number of nodes, will be recognized as an error condition by all other nodes in the network. In turn they, too, will send an error frame to the bus.

The actual posting of the error frames may occur at different times from node to node. As a result, the actual error flag, as it occurs on the bus, may be constructed by a superposition of several error frames.

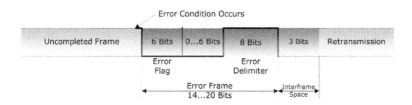

Picture 4.7.2: "Realistic" Error Frame Architecture

As shown in picture 4.7.2, the actual error flag length will be between 6 and 12 bit times. The total error frame length will be between 14 and 20 bit times. Using these numbers plus the Interframe Space length of 3 bits it is possible to determine the total error recovery time in a CAN network.

Error Frame Length	Baud Rate	Total Error Recovery Time [Error Frame + Interframe Space]
14 bits	1 MBit/sec	14 + 3 µsec
	500 kBit/sec	28 + 6 µsec
	250 kBit/sec	56 + 12 µsec
20 bits	1 MBit/sec	20 + 3 µsec
	500 kBit/sec	40 + 6 µsec
	250 kBit/sec	80 + 12 µsec

Table 4.7.1: Error Recovery Times

Such short error recovery times are one of the many advantages of CAN when compared to other fieldbus protocols.

As shown in table 4.7.1 the error recovery time in a CAN network is very short; the actual time depends primarily on the chosen baud rate, but also on the actual bit length of the error frame.

In order to prevent a defective node from continuously reporting errors and therefore blocking the entire CAN bus, the CAN standard defines two different error reporting rights, error-active and error-passive. Such a defective node will switch from error-active to error-passive mode and, unless the node was repaired, eventually will remove itself from the bus (self-retirement). A transmitting, but error-passive node can report the termination of its own message to the bus, but it cannot destroy any message it received from other nodes (see also Chapter 8 - Error Detection and Fault Confinement).

4.7.1   ERROR FLAG

A node, that detects an error, will send an error frame, starting with the error flag. This occurs immediately with the next bit interval, unless the detected error is a CRC error.

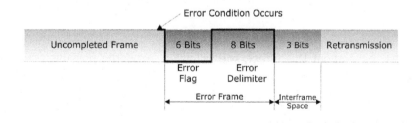

Picture 4.7.1.1: Basic Error Frame Architecture

In case of a CRC error the sending of the error flag will be delayed by two bit times in order not to conflict with the Acknowledge function (see picture 4.7.1.2).

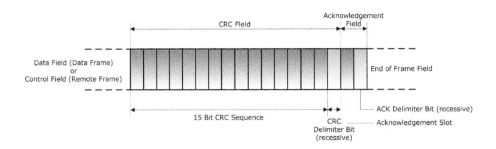

Picture 4.7.1.2: CRC and Acknowledgement Field

As mentioned in the previous chapter, the actual error flag, as it occurs on the bus, may be constructed by a superposition of several error frames.

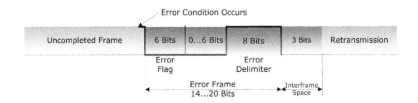

Picture 4.7.1.3: "Realistic" Error Frame

To elaborate a bit more about this effect, the following are some possible error detecting and reporting scenarios:

> **Example: Transmitting Error**
> Picture 4.7.1.4 demonstrates the scenario of a local transmitting error. The transmitting node in a CAN network detects, for instance, a data bit error (see also

Chapter 8.1 - Error Detection) and immediately, with the beginning of the next bit interval, starts the transmission of the error frame, starting with the error flag.

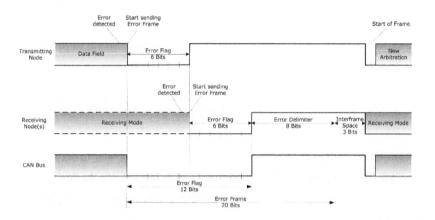

Picture 4.7.1.4: Example 1 - Super Positioning of Error Frames

Each transmitting node in a CAN network compares its output signal with the actual bus level at the end of each bit cycle (Bit Monitoring). An error will be reported, should the comparison show different levels.
(see also Chapter 8.1 - Error Detection).

Picture 4.7.1.4 also demonstrates how a receiving node (actually each other node in the network) reacts to a *Bit Stuffing Error*, i.e. the sequence of more than 5 consecutive bits of the same level.

As a result of the bit stuffing violation the receiving node(s) will post an error frame as well. The super positioning of both error flags reflects to the bus as shown in the picture. In this example the error flag has a length of 12 bits; the total error frame length is 20 bits.

Following the Error Delimiter (8 bits) and the Interframe Space (3 bits) output by the other node(s) in the network, the transmitting node will engage into another bus arbitration cycle.

The question, however, is, how does the node know <u>when</u> to output the new Start of Frame signal? After all, it had sent out the 6 bit long error flag and, after another 11 bits (error delimiter and Interframe space), the node might consider the bus idle and start the new arbitration right then. This would, of course, cause a confusion on the CAN bus.

The answer to this question lies in the initial posting of the Error Delimiter as explained in *Chapter 4.7.2 - Error Delimiter.*

The next error detecting and reporting example describes a receiving error scenario:

> **Example: Receiving Error**
> A message transmitting node monitors the bus and expects a dominant level during the ACK slot. This will be the case when either one of the other CAN nodes outputs a dominant level.

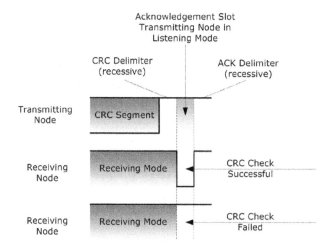

Picture 4.7.1.5: Acknowledgement Function

In this sample scenario, one of the receiving nodes in the network detects a check sum (CRC Sequence) error (see also *Chapter 8.1 - Error Detection*) and immediately, with the beginning of the next bit interval, starts the transmission of the error frame, starting with the error flag (see picture 4.7.1.6).

In case of a CRC error the sending of the error flag will be delayed by two bit times in order not to conflict with the Acknowledge function (See picture 4.7.1.2).

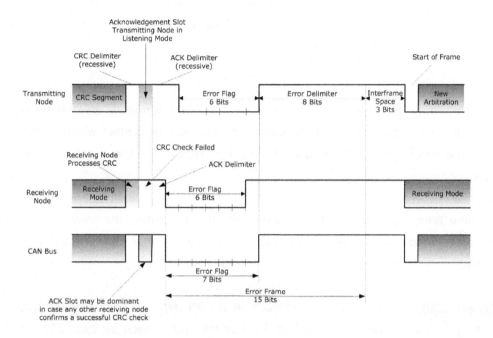

Picture 4.7.1.6: Example 2 - Super Positioning of Error Frames

Picture 4.7.1.6 demonstrates the output levels of a transmitting and a receiving node, which in turn detects the CRC error, and the actual bus level.

The transmitting node, after sending the CRC sequence plus the recessive CRC Delimiter, will switch into listening (receiving) mode and wait for one bit time to monitor the response from other nodes in the network. In this example a receiving node determined a CRC error during the CRC Delimiter and reports the error by posting a recessive level during the Acknowledgement Slot. The posting of the recessive level may not have any effect on the bus level in case other nodes in the network do not detect a CRC error. In this case the bus level will remain dominant.

Hear Ye! Hear Ye!

The CAN standard takes into consideration that a defective node may detect errors while the other nodes in the network do not see a problem. In order to prevent a defective node from continuously reporting errors and therefore blocking the entire CAN bus, the CAN standard defines two different error reporting rights, error-active and error-passive (see also Chapter 8 - Error Detection and Fault Confinement).

The error reporting node will delay the posting of an error frame for two bit times, i.e. the Acknowledgement slot and the ACK Delimiter, in order not to conflict with the Acknowledge function. The error frame will be sent to the bus right after the completion of the ACK Delimiter.

At the same time, i.e. right after the completed ACK Delimiter, the transmitting node will detect a bit error, because it was attempting to send the first of 7 recessive bits of the End of Frame field.

Each transmitting node in a CAN network compares its output signal with the actual bus level at the end of each bit cycle (Bit Monitoring). An error will be reported, should the comparison show different levels. (see also Chapter 8.1 - Error Detection).

The transmitting node in turn will post its own error frame. As shown in picture 4.7.1.6 the resulting error flag length on the bus will be 7 bit times.

Both examples, transmitting and receiving error, describe scenarios of overlapping error flags posted by different nodes in the network. The CAN standard considers the monitoring and timing of error frames to determine which node(s) reported the error first. In addition the determination of local and global errors allows the detection of single defective nodes (see Chapter 8 - Error Detection and Fault Confinement).

4.7.2   ERROR DELIMITER

Per definition the error delimiter is represented by a sequence of 8 recessive bits. An error reporting node, after completing the Error Flag, will send the first recessive bit to the bus. By means of bit monitoring the node will continue sending a recessive level until the bus actually turns recessive.

Eventually, all nodes in the network will output a recessive level to the bus and wait until the bus is recessive as well. That can only be the case when all nodes have finished sending their individual Error Flag and have sent the first bit of their individual Error Delimiter. As soon as the bus is recessive, all nodes will continue with sending the remaining 7 bits of the Error Delimiter.

This algorithm is used to synchronize all nodes towards the first bit of the Error Delimiter and consequently to the next possible Start of Frame bit.

It also allows a node to determine whether or not it was the first error reporting node, which in turn allows the determination and consequently the removal of defective nodes.

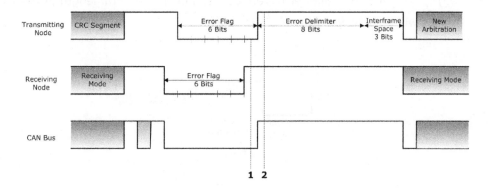

Picture 4.7.2.1: Receiving Error Example

Picture 4.7.2.1 refers to the Receiving Error example as described in the previous chapter (See also picture 4.7.1.6).

In this scenario two nodes are sending an error frame, including the error delimiter, at different times:

1 The receiving node outputs a recessive level (first of 8 recessive bits of the error delimiter) to the bus and through bit monitoring detects a dominant level, which determines that the receiving node was the first to detect and report an error.

2 The transmitting node outputs a recessive level (first of 8 recessive bits of the error delimiter) to the bus. Through bit monitoring it detects a recessive level and thus continues to send the remaining 7 bits.

4.8 OVERLOAD FRAME

An Overload Frame is a special version of an Error Frame, but unlike an Error Frame is does not cause the retransmission of the previous frame. Just like the error frame it contains of a 6-Bit flag (Overload Flag), that can expand up to 12 bits on the bus (see *Chapter 4.8.1 - Overload Flag*)[16], and an 8-Bit delimiter (Overload Delimiter). The total length of the Overload Frame on the bus will be between 14 and 20 bit times.

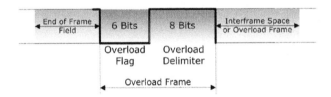

Picture 4.8.1: Basic Overload Frame Architecture

A node can request a delay between two Data or Remote Frames, meaning the Overload Frame can only occur between Data or Remote Frame transmissions.

---

[16] The variable length of the Overload Flag due to super positioning of several Overload Flags is mentioned in the original Bosch specification, but the document fails to make exact statements. The super positioning is not at all mentioned in the ISO 11898-1 standard.

As its name indicates, the Overload Frame is transmitted by a node that is temporarily "overloaded" and will not be able to participate in any CAN bus communication. As a result the ransmission of a Data or Remote Frame by any node in the network will be delayed until the end of the Overload Frame.

In addition the Overload Frame is used to report the following error conditions (Reactive Overload Frame):

➢ Detection of a dominant bit during the first two bits of the Interframe Space
➢ Detection of a dominant bit in the last bit of the End of Frame field by a receiver
➢ Detection of a dominant bit by any node at the last bit of an Error Delimiter or Overload Delimiter.

An Overload Frame, requesting the delay of the next transmission, will start with the first bit of an Interframe (Intermission) Field. The 6 bit long Overload Flag will consequently override the 3 recessive bits of the Intermission Field. A Reactive Overload Frame will start one bit after detecting a dominant bit according to the conditions listed above. At most, two Overload Frames may be generated to delay the next Data Frame or Remote Frame.

Picture 4.8.2 demonstrates the similarity between an Error Frame and an Overload Frame. The Overload Frame can only occur between Data or Remote Frame transmissions, right after the End of Frame field of the last transmitted frame, while the Error Frame occurs only during a Data or Remote Frame.

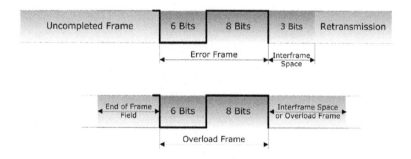

Picture 4.8.2: Comparison Error and Overload Frame

4.8.1   OVERLOAD FLAG[17]

The Overload Flag consists of six consecutive dominant bits. It destroys the fixed format of the Interframe Space. Consequently, all other nodes in the network will detect an overload condition (see error detection list in previous chapter) and, too, start sending an Overload Flag. This will effectively stop all message traffic in the network.

Just like the Error Flag, the Overload Flag, as it appears on the bus, may be between 6 and 12 bits long, due to super positioning of Overload Flags sent by other nodes in the network.

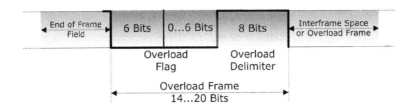

Picture 4.8.1.1: "Realistic" Overload Frame Architecture

In all actuality the Overload Flag length on the bus can never be limited to six bits, unless all nodes in the network request a delay at the same time.

Picture 4.8.1.2 demonstrates a scenario where one node requests a delay by sending an Overload Frame.

---

[17] Statements regarding the actual Overload Flag length on the bus are solely derived from descriptions in the Bosch CAN specification. However, the document fails to provide exact bit numbers. The ISO 11898-1 standard does not mention the super positioning of Overload Flags at all. Other documents are at best vague or are just plain wrong.

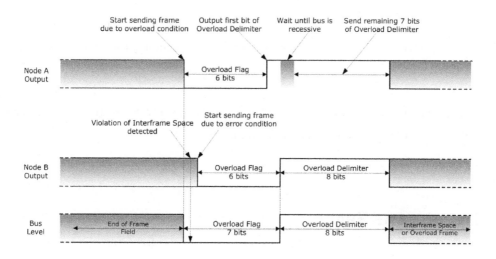

Picture 4.8.1.2: Overload Frame Example

The second node in the network reacts to a violation of the frame format, i.e. it detected a dominant bit during the first two bits of the Interframe Space. In turn it will report an error by sending another Overload Frame to the bus. The sending of the frame is delayed by one bit time, i.e. the error was detected during the first bit of the Interframe Space and is reported at the beginning of the next bit. In this scenario the Overload Flag will have a length of 7 bits on the bus.

4.8.2 OVERLOAD DELIMITER

The Overload Delimiter consists of eight consecutive recessive bits. As was previously explained the Overload Frame is posted by one node requesting a delay of sending the next Data Frame or Remote Frame. All other nodes in the network will react and report a violation within the first two bits of the Interframe Space. The requesting node will send the first bit of the Overload Delimiter after completing the output of the six bit Overload Flag. By means of bit monitoring the node will continue sending a recessive level until the bus actually turns recessive.

Eventually, all nodes in the network will output a recessive level to the bus and wait until the bus is recessive as well. That can only be the case when all nodes have finished sending their individual Overload Flag and have sent the first bit of their individual Overload Delimiter. As soon as the bus is recessive, all nodes will continue with sending the remaining 7 bits of the Overload Delimiter.

This algorithm is used to synchronize all nodes towards the first bit of the Error Delimiter and consequently to the next possible Start of Frame bit.

4.9 INTERFRAME SPACE

The Interframe Space represents the minimum space between frames of any type (data, remote, error, overload) and a following data or remote frame. During the Interframe Space (intermission) no node can start the transmission of a data or remote frame. Only the signaling of an overload condition is allowed (see *Chapter 4.8 - Overload Frame*).

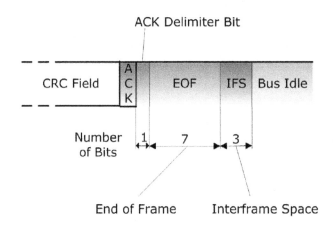

Picture 4.9.1: Interframe Space

There is no Interframe space between error and overload frames. The Interframe Space can not necessarily be considered to be a part of a data or remote frame, however, in a well functioning CAN network it will always follow behind a data or remote frame.

4.10 FRAME LENGTH AND TRANSMISSION TIMES

The transmission time of a CAN data or remote frame depends, first of all, on the baud rate (i.e. the transmission speed in bit/sec) and its actual length (number of bits).

Since a remote frame is basically a data frame with no data, its frame bit size depends only on the message ID length and the number of stuff bits. The frame bit length of a data frame depends on the size of the data field (up to 8 bytes = 64 bit), the message ID length and the number of stuff bits.

The following tables provide an overview of frame lengths and transmission times based on an 11 bit message ID and an average number of stuff bits. An 11 bit identifier can be considered a standard in the automation industry. A 29 bit identifier is primarily applied in vehicles that make use of the SAE J1939 higher layer protocol (see also *Chapter 3.5 - Higher Layer Protocols*).

Table 4.10.1 lists the bit lengths of a remote frame (0 data bytes) and a data frame (8 data bytes as an example).

	Data Field 0 Bytes	Data Field 8 Bytes
No bit stuffing	47 bits	111 bits
Max. bit stuffing (worst case scenario)	55 bits	135 bits
Average bit stuffing	49 bits	114 bits

Table 4.10.1: Frame Lengths (11-Bit Identifier)

The average bit stuffing value has been determined in an extensive simulation study with random data fields (see also *Chapter 7.2 - Bit Stuffing*). Table 4.10.2 shows the total frame times and the maximum number of messages per second based on the bit lengths as shown in table 4.10.1, but using the average bit stuffing.

Data Bytes	Frame Length	Baud Rate	Total Frame Time	Max. messages/sec
0	49 bits*	1 MBit/sec	49 μsec	20,408
		500 kBit/sec	98 μsec	10,204
		250 kBit/sec	196 μsec	5,102
8	114 bits*	1 MBit/sec	114 μsec	8,771
		500 kBit/sec	228 μsec	4,385
		250 kBit/sec	456 μsec	2,192

Table 4.10.2: Transmission Times (11-Bit Identifier)

* Average bit stuffing is applied (see also *Chapter 7.2 - Bit Stuffing*).

4.11 BAUD RATE CONSIDERATIONS

Another frequently asked question addresses the choice of a proper baud rate for the various applications. First of all, the user must consider that a maximum baud rate of 1 MBit/sec limits the maximum bus length to roughly 120 feet (40 meters).

Bit Rate [kBit/sec]	Nominal Bit-Time [μsec]	Bus Length [ft] / [m]
1000	1	120 / 40
500	2	360 / 110
250	4	920 / 280
125	8	2030 / 620

Table 4.11.1: Baud rates, bit times, bus length

Table 4.11.1 shows a sample list of baud rates, the bit times and the resulting bus length. For more detailed information on bus length consideration see also *Chapter 9.6 - Maximum Bus Length*.

It is estimated that the vast majority of CAN applications, even including real-time demanding motion control tasks, will function without noticeable restrictions at baud rates of 500 kBit/sec.

Hear Ye! Hear Ye!

Consider for your application: The maximum number of CAN messages per second is 8,771 (at 1 MBit/sec, 8 bytes per message), up to 17,543 at 1 MBit/sec and 1 byte per message (average bit stuffing applied). This results into a data transfer between 17,543 and 70,168 data bytes per second.

The **CiA Draft Standard** DS-102 recommends the following baud rates:[18]

Bit Rate [kBit/sec]	Nominal Bit Time [µsec]
1000	1
800	1.25
500	2
250	4
125	8
100[19]	10
50	20
20	50
10	100

Table 4.11.2: CiA Baud Rate Recommendations

---

[18] DS-102 is a mere 5 page document that, besides the recommended pin assignment of a CAN connector and CAN baud rates, contains primarily references to documents such as the Bosch CAN Specification, ISO 11898, and others.
[19] DS-102 remarks: "Not recommended for new developments" with no further explanation.

4.12 BANDWIDTH

Bandwidth is the amount of data that can be transferred over a network in a defined amount of time. In a CAN network, it is usually expressed in bits per second (bps). Bandwidth should not be confused with the term band, such as a wireless phone that operates on the 800 MHz band. In this case bandwidth is the space it occupies on that band.

The maximum bandwidth under CAN is, of course, 1 MBit per second, however, this particular number does not sufficiently describe the amount of raw data being transmitted over a certain time.

 *The maximum number of CAN messages per second is 8,771 (at 1 MBit/sec, 8 bytes per message), up to 17,543 at 1 MBit/sec and 1 byte per message (average bit stuffing applied). This results in a data transfer between 17,543 and 70,168 data bytes per second.*

As any other serial fieldbus system, CAN has to live with a certain amount of protocol overhead. In case of a CAN data message frame the "protocol overhead" is represented by the bits prior to the data field as well as the bits following the data field.

The definition of the exact "net" CAN bandwidth, i.e. the number of real data bits or bytes per time unit, depends on many factors such as used baud rate, number of bytes per data message frame, the number of remote frames used and the occurrence of error conditions (which can only be assumed for worst case scenario determination).

Another look at a typical CAN message frame with an 11-Bit message identifier is shown in picture 4.12.1.

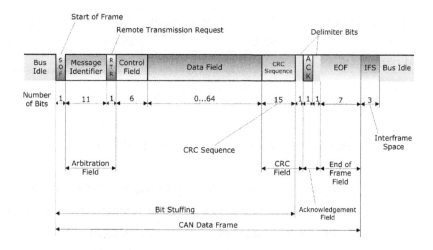

Picture 4.12.1: Detailed Data Frame Architecture

The total frame length is between 47 bits (0 data bytes = Remote Frame) and 111 bits (8 data bytes).

Description	Number of Bits	
SOF	1	
Arbitration Field	12	
Control Field	6	19 Bits preceding data
Data Field	0...64	0...64 data bits
CRC Field	16	
ACK Field	2	
End of Frame Field	7	
Interframe Space	3	28 Bits succeeding data

Table 4.12.1: CAN Protocol Overhead (11-Bit Identifier)

The actual bandwidth use can be calculated by dividing the number of actual data bits by the total frame length.

Number of data bytes	Total Frame Length	Bandwidth Usage
1 (8 bits)	57 bits*	14 %
8 (64 bits)	114 bits*	56 %

Table 4.12.2: Bandwidth Usage (11-Bit Identifier)

* Average bit stuffing is applied (see also *Chapter 7.2 - Bit Stuffing*).

As shown in table 4.12.2 the maximum bandwidth use (using an 11-Bit identifier) is 56%. This number does not take into consideration the occurrence of remote, error, or overload frames. Consequently, the realistic bandwidth usage will be somewhat less than 56%.

All bandwidth usage calculations so far were based on an 11 bit message identifier, which can be considered a standard in the automation industry. A 29 bit identifier is primarily applied in vehicles that make use of the SAE J1939 higher layer protocol (see also *Chapter 3.5 - Higher Layer Protocols*).

The extended format (29-Bit message identifier) has some trade-offs: The bus latency time is longer (minimum 20 bit-times); messages in extended format require more bandwidth (about 20 %), and the error detection performance is reduced (because the chosen polynomial for the 15-bit CRC is optimized for frame length up to 112 bits).

As was described in *Chapter 4.6 - Extended CAN Protocol*, the arbitration field of a CAN message using a 29-Bit message identifier is extended from 12 to 32 bits (see picture 4.12.2).

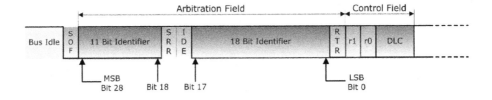

Picture 4.12.2: Arbitration Field with 29-Bit Message Identifier

The total frame length is between 67 bits (0 data bytes = Remote Frame) and 131 bits (8 data bytes).

Description	Number of Bits	
SOF	1	
Arbitration Field	32	
Control Field	6	39 Bits preceding data
Data Field	0...64	0...64 data bits
CRC Field	16	
ACK Field	2	
End of Frame Field	7	
Interframe Space	3	28 Bits succeeding data

Table 4.12.3 : CAN Protocol Overhead (29-Bit Identifier)

The actual bandwidth use can be calculated by dividing the number of actual data bits by the total frame length.

Number of data bytes	Total Frame Length	Bandwidth Usage
1 (8 bits)	78 bits*	10 %
8 (64 bits)	135 bits*	47 %

Table 4.12.4: Bandwidth Usage (29-Bit Identifier)

* Average bit stuffing is applied (see also *Chapter 7.2 - Bit Stuffing*).

As shown in table 4.12.4 the maximum bandwidth use (using an 29-Bit identifier) is 47%. This number does not take into consideration the occurrence of remote, error, or overload frames. Consequently, the realistic bandwidth usage will be somewhat less than 47%.

Chapter

5

MESSAGE BROADCASTING

The broadcasting of messages in a CAN network is based on a producer-consumer principle. One node, when sending a message, will be the producer while all other nodes are the consumers. All nodes in a CAN network receive the same message at the same time.

In a multi-master network nodes may transmit data at any time. Each node "listens" to the network bus and will receive every transmitted message. The CAN protocol supports message-filtering, i.e. the receiving nodes will only react to data that is relevant to them.

Messages in CAN are not confirmed, because that would unnecessarily increase the bus traffic. CAN assumes that all messages are compliant with the defined standard and if they do not, there will be a corresponding response by all nodes in the network (see *Chapter 8.1 - Error Detection*). All receiving nodes check the consistency of the received frame and acknowledge the consistency. If the consistency is not acknowledged by any or all nodes in the network, the transmitter of the frame will post an error message to the bus.

If either one or more nodes are unable to decode a message, i.e. either detect an error in the message or are unable to read the message due to an internal malfunction, the entire bus will be notified of the error condition. Nodes that transmit faulty data or nodes that are constantly unable to receive a message correctly remove themselves from the bus (see *Chapter 8.3 - Fault Confinement*) and thus allow restoration of proper bus conditions.

The CAN standard also defines the request of a transmission from another node by means of a remote frame. The remote frame and the requested data frame use the same message identifier. They are, however, distinguished by the RTR bit (Remote Transmission Request) during the arbitration process (see also *Chapter 4 - Message Frame Architecture*).

The following will explain with examples the two methods of message broadcasting, data frame and remote frame broadcasting.

5.1 MESSAGE BROADCASTING WITH DATA FRAMES

Per definition, CAN nodes are not concerned with information about the system configuration (e.g. node address), hence CAN does not support node IDs. Instead, receivers process messages by means of an acceptance filtering process, which decides whether the received message is relevant for node's application layer or not. There is no need for the receiver to know the transmitter of the information and vice versa.

All nodes in a CAN network receive the same message at the same time, meaning each node "listens" to the network bus and will receive every transmitted message. The message filter guarantees that the receiving nodes will only react to data that is relevant to them.

Picture 5.1.1 demonstrates the message broadcasting of a data frame, in this case in a four node CAN network. It also provides a first, but very rudimentary look into the architecture of a CAN controller. Each node represents a CAN controller, which, among many other function blocks, accommodates a programmable message filter and a message buffer.

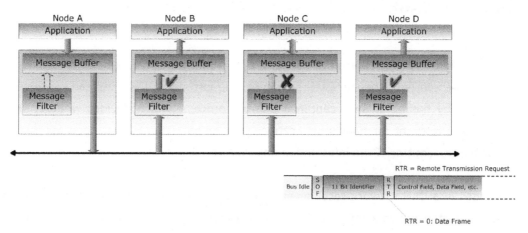

Picture 5.1.1: Data Frame Transmission

Note that a data frame is recognized by a dominant RTR (Remote Transmission Request) bit (refer to *Chapter 4 - Message Frame Architecture*).

The data transmission/reception sequence is as follows (example):
- ➤ Node A transmits a message
- ➤ Nodes B, C and D receive the message
- ➤ Nodes B and D accept the message, Node C declines

This example demonstrates very clearly how flexible the broadcasting of messages can be.

 *The definition of message IDs and the setup of the message filter depends solely on the application needs. Message IDs must be assigned during the design phase and are usually hard-coded into the application.*

5.2 MESSAGE REQUEST WITH REMOTE FRAMES

Per definition, CAN nodes are not concerned with information about the system configuration (e.g. node address), hence CAN does not support node IDs. Instead, receivers process messages by means of an acceptance filtering process, which decides whether the received message is relevant for node's application layer or not. There is no need for the receiver to know the transmitter of the information and vice versa.

All nodes in a CAN network receive the same message at the same time, meaning each node "listens" to the network bus and will receive every transmitted message. The message filter guarantees that the receiving nodes will only react to data that is relevant to them.

Picture 5.2.1 demonstrates the message broadcasting of a remote frame, in this case in a four node CAN network.

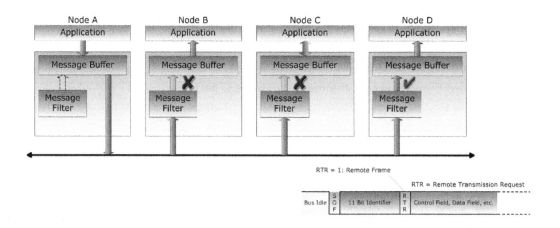

Picture 5.2.1: Message Request per Remote Frame

Note that a remote frame is recognized by a recessive RTR (Remote Transmission Request) bit (refer to *Chapter 4 - Message Frame Architecture*).

The message request sequence is as follows (example):

> ➢ Node A sends a remote frame to request data
> ➢ Node B, C and D receive the message
> ➢ Node D accepts the message, Nodes B and C decline

The data request cycle in a CAN network will involve the sending of two messages, the actual message request (remote frame), followed by the requested data (data frame).

It may be obvious, but it is important to know that the sending of a remote frame, meaning the request of a data frame, consequently causes a response, namely the sending of a data frame containing the requested information.

Picture 5.2.2 demonstrates in a further example the response to the remote frame, i.e. the sending of a data frame.

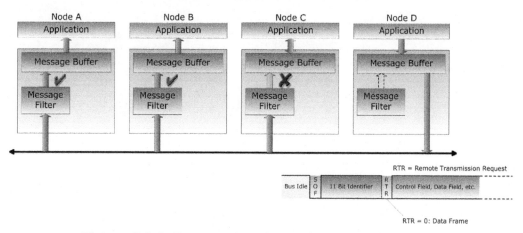

Picture 5.2.2: Transmission of requested message

Note that a data frame is recognized by a dominant RTR (Remote Transmission Request) bit (refer to *Chapter 4 - Message Frame Architecture*).

The data transmission/reception sequence is as follows (example):
> ➢ Node D sends the requested message
> ➢ Nodes A, B and C receive the requested message
> ➢ Nodes A and B accept the requested message, Node C declines

The definition of message IDs and the setup of the message filter depend solely on the application needs. Message IDs must be assigned during the design phase and are usually hard-coded into the application.

Hear Ye! Hear Ye!

The remote frame and the requested data frame use the same message identifier. Both frames are distinguished by the RTR (Remote Transmission Request) bit, which is part of the arbitration field. In case a data frame and a remote frame using the same message ID try to access the bus simultaneously, the data frame will gain the bus access over the remote frame, since it uses a dominant RTR bit.

Chapter 6

Bus Arbitration

Since a serial communication system such as CAN is based on a two-wire connection between nodes in the network, i.e. all nodes are sharing the same physical communication bus, a method of message/data collision avoidance is mandatory to assure a safe data transfer and to avoid delays resulting from the necessary restoration of proper bus conditions after the collision.

A collision may occur when two or more nodes in the network are attempting to access the bus at virtually the same time, which may result in unwelcome effects, such as bus access delays or even destruction/damage of messages.

There are various methods of collision avoidance between the various fieldbus systems and in most cases the collision avoidance is actually a collision "repair", which requires an unspecified bus recovery time, therefore taking up valuable bandwidth, and usually results in the destruction of the message.

CAN averts message/data collisions by using the message ID of the node, i.e. the message with the highest priority (= lowest message ID) will gain access to the bus, while all other nodes (with lower priority message IDs) switch to a "listening" mode.

Not only is the CAN arbitration cycle accomplished in a predictable, i.e. constant, time, the CAN specification also guarantees that low-priority messages who lost the arbitration will start a new arbitration as soon as the bus is available again. Thus CAN provides a non-destructive bus arbitration.

6.1 PRINCIPLE OF BUS ARBITRATION

Chapter 4 - Message Frame Architecture explains the detailed structure of a CAN message frame bit by bit. Picture 6.1.1 provides a closer look into the arbitration field of a CAN message, in this case a CAN message with an 11 Bit identifier.

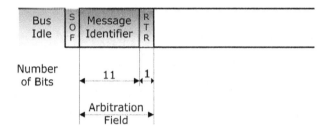

Picture 6.1.1: Arbitration Field

The arbitration field follows right after the SOF (Start of Frame) bit and it contains of the message ID and the RTR (Remote Transmission Request) bit.

Per definition, CAN nodes are not concerned with information about the system configuration (e.g. node address), hence CAN does not support node IDs. CAN data transmissions are distinguished by a unique message identifier (11/29 bit), which also represents the message priority. A low message ID represents a high priority.

High priority messages will gain bus access within shortest time even when the bus load is high caused by lower priority messages.

Picture 6.1.2 shows an example where three nodes in a four node CAN network try to access the bus at virtually the same time. In this example node C will win the bus access within 12 clock times. At a baud rate of 1 MBit/sec this would translate into 12 microseconds. Naturally, the bus arbitration time varies with baud rate and the message identifier length, 11 or 29 Bit.

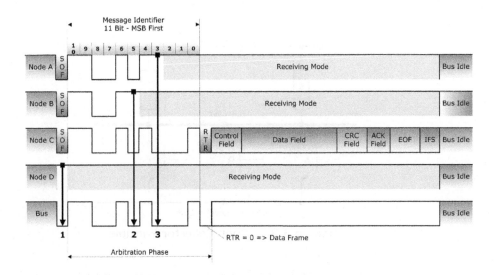

Picture 6.1.2: Bus Arbitration Example

Before engaging into a detailed explanation of the arbitration process as shown in this example, it is important to lay out the ground rules on which bus arbitration works.

6.2 MAIN RULES OF BUS ARBITRATION

The main rules of bus arbitration are:

> Bit wise arbitration across the Arbitration Field
> Zero Bit = Dominant Bus Level, One Bit = Recessive Bus Level, dominant bit overrides recessive bit

The CAN bus level will be dominant in case any number of nodes in the network output a dominant level. The CAN bus level will only be recessive when all nodes in the network output a recessive level.

An equivalent from some electronics basics will explain the relationship between node output and the resulting bus level as shown in picture 6.2.1.

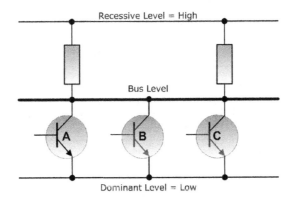

Picture 6.2.1: Open Collector Principle

This example uses three nodes in a CAN network, in this case represented by three transistors in open-collector configuration ("Wired And"). The bus level will be at low level (dominant) in case any number of transistors in the network output a dominant level. The bus level will only be at high level (recessive) when all transistors in the network output a recessive level.

Node			
A	B	C	Bus
0	0	0	0
0	0	1	0
0	1	0	0
0	1	1	0
1	0	0	0
1	0	1	0
1	1	0	0
1	1	1	1

Table 6.2.1: Wired And

> ➤ Bus is considered idle, i.e. free for access, after end of the completely transmitted message followed by the Intermission Field.

> ➤ Node that transmits message with lowest message ID, i.e. highest priority, wins the arbitration and continues to transmit. Competing nodes switch to receiving mode (listening mode).

> ➤ Nodes that lost arbitration will start a new arbitration as soon as the bus is free for access (idle) again. Thus CAN provides a non-destructive bus arbitration.

Picture 6.2.2 demonstrates the interaction between a CAN node, trying to access the bus, and the actual CAN bus.

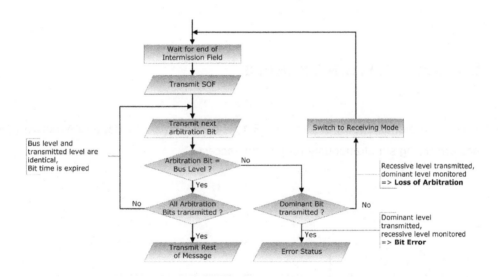

Picture 6.2.2: Arbitration Process Flow Chart

1. The CAN node (CAN controller) waits for the end of the intermission field (refer to *Chapter 4 - Message Frame Architecture*).
2. As soon as the bus is being detected as idle, the CAN node signals an SOF (Start of Frame) by putting a dominant (low) level onto the bus. Every other node in the network, that did not request bus access, will immediately switch to a receiving mode.

3. The CAN controller sends the first/next message ID bit (Message IDs can be 11 or 29 bit long, the most significant bit – MSB will be sent first).

4. The CAN controller compares its output signal with the actual bus level (at the end of each bit cycle).

5. The node will lose the arbitration, in case it did send a recessive level (high) and detects a dominant (low) bus level. Consequently the node will switch into receiving mode.

6. An error condition exists when the node detects a recessive level on the bus after it did output a dominant level. This is a clear violation of the CAN standard and the node will send an error frame to the bus.

7. If the node has finished sending all arbitration bits (message ID plus RTR) without loosing the bus arbitration, it will transmit the rest of the message. At this time all other CAN nodes in the network will have switched to receiving mode.

6.3 BUS ARBITRATION EXAMPLE

The following example, as shown in picture 6.3.1, is based on a four node CAN network, where three nodes are trying simultaneously to gain bus access.

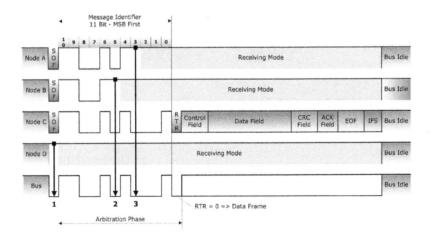

Picture 6.3.1: Bus Arbitration Example

The nodes in this example have the following message IDs:

A   1100101100 = 32C hex

B   1100110000 = 330 hex

C   1100101000 = 328 hex

The message ID of node D is of no significance, since it is not requesting bus access. According to this example and the CAN specification (lowest message ID represents highest message priority) node C must gain the bus access.

The sequence of the bus arbitration process in this example is as follows:

1   • Nodes A, B and C request bus access at the same time by putting a dominant level to the bus (SOF = Start of Frame). Node D, not requesting bus access, will switch immediately to receiving mode.

    • Nodes A, B and C output their message ID bits starting with the most significant bit (MSB).

2   • Between the transmission of bit 10 and bit 6 of the message ID there is no difference in signal level.

    • After transmission of bit 5 node B loses the bus arbitration, since nodes A and C are posting a dominant level and node B posts a recessive level. Node B switches to receiving mode.

3   • After transmission of bit 3 node A loses the bus arbitration, since it posts a recessive level to the bus, which is overridden by a dominant level from node C.

    • Node C gains the bus access and continues with the transmission of the remainder of the message.

Chapter

7

DATA TRANSFER SYNCHRONIZATION

There may be numerous nodes in a CAN network with each node using its own time reference provided by their individual oscillators. There is no guarantee that all oscillators in the network will be running absolutely synchronous. As a matter of fact, there will be oscillator tolerances, due to environmental factors such as temperature or humidity, etc., and they need to be compensated.

The falling (leading) edge of the SOF bit (transition from recessive to dominant bus level), sent by the first node that attempts to access the bus, serves as a mechanism to synchronize all CAN bus nodes.

The CAN data transfer provides only limited means for a "hard" synchronization of the bit stream, namely the falling edge of the Start-Of-Frame Bit. The CAN bit stream is transmitted based on the Non-Return-to-Zero bit coding principle, which provides a maximum of transport capacity, but in turn lacks a sufficient number of signal edges for synchronization.

In order to compensate for the lack of signal edges the CAN standard incorporated mechanisms such as:

- ➢ **Bit Stuffing** to create a sufficient number of signal edges
- ➢ **Continuous Resynchronization** of the bit sample point

7.1 BIT CODING

There are various methods of bit coding, such as Non-Return-to-Zero (NRZ), Manchester, Pulse Width Modulation, and others, which can be distinguished by the number of necessary clock times per bit.

The effect of bit coding according to Non-Return-to-Zero principle (NRZ bit coding) is that the bit level remains constant during the entire bit time (See example in picture 7.1.1), which, however, posts a node synchronization problem during the transmission of larger bit blocks of the same polarity.

Picture 7.1.1: Sample bit stream according to NRZ bit coding

The Manchester bit coding, for instance, is designed in a way that it provides an edge, raising ("0" level) or falling ("1" level), during each bit time, which provides sufficient signal edges for synchronization between sender and receiver.

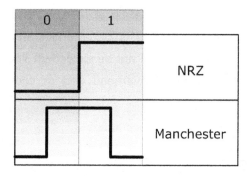

Picture 7.1.2: Comparison NRZ and Manchester bit coding

As demonstrated in picture 7.1.3, the Manchester bit coding also limits the transport capacity by requiring higher frequencies (actually twice the frequency) for the same baud rate (bits per second).

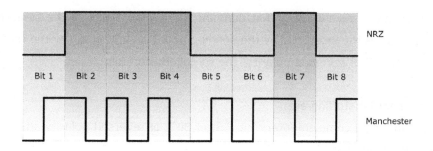

Picture 7.1.3: Sample bit stream, NRZ and Manchester

Bit Coding according to Non-Return-to-Zero principle:

- Provides highest transport capacity
- Has constant bit level over bit time
- Lacks sufficient signal edges for synchronization of bit stream
- Requires "Bit Stuffing"
- Requires additional continuous bit synchronization

Bit Stuffing, i.e. the insertion of an additional bit of reversed polarity after a series of bits of the same polarity, provides a higher number of signal edges and assures that the maximum allowable time between two signal edges will not be exceeded. The downside, however, is that Bit Stuffing increases the CAN protocol overhead and in consequence reduces the data bandwidth.

7.2 BIT STUFFING

The CAN standard allows only 5 consecutive bits of the same polarity between the SOF bit and (including) the CRC Field of a message frame; every bit stream of more than 5 bits of the same polarity, dominant or recessive, is considered an error condition. As a matter of fact, CAN uses this rule to send an error frame, which contains of (minimum) 6 consecutive dominant bits. Each node in the network will recognize the violation of the standard and initiate appropriate responses.

In order to transmit or receive data that contains more than 5 bits of the same polarity the CAN standard requires the insertion (by the sending node) and filtering (by the receiving node) of a complimentary bit of reversed polarity, the so-called Stuff Bit.

The ground rules for bit stuffing are:
- Sender inserts a complementary Bit ("Stuff Bit") of reversed polarity after 5 successive Bits of the same level
- Receiver filters the complementary Bit
- Bit stuffing is not allowed in the static format fields of a CAN frame

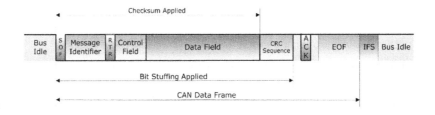

Picture 7.2.1: Bit Stuffing Range

Bit stuffing is **allowed** in the following fields of a CAN message frame:

> ➢ Start of Frame
>
> ➢ Arbitration Field
>
> ➢ Control Field
>
> ➢ Data Field
>
> ➢ CRC Sequence

Bit Stuffing is **not allowed** in the static fields of a CAN message frame:

> ➢ CRC Delimiter
>
> ➢ Acknowledgement Field
>
> ➢ End of Frame Field
>
> ➢ Intermission Field

(see also *Chapter 4 - Message Frame Architecture*)

 *Error and Overload Frames are transmitted without Bit Stuffing.*

The advantages of bit stuffing are:

> ➢ Bit stuffing provides additional signal edges for data transfer synchronization after 5 Bits
>
> ➢ Bit stuffing provides the means to signal and cause an error frame (see *Chapter 4.7 - Error Frame*)

Picture 7.2.2 demonstrates the use of a stuff bit:

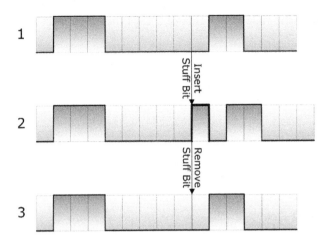

Picture 7.2.2: Bit Stuffing Example

1. Bit sequence to be transmitted
2. Transmitted Bit sequence on bus after bit stuffing
3. Bit sequence at receiver after filtering Stuff Bit

There is a special case where the stuff bit actually contributes to the building of a 5 bit sequence, which in turn requires an additional stuff bit.

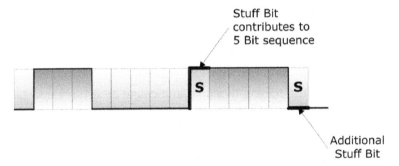

Picture 7.2.2: Additional Bit Stuffing

The example as shown in picture 7.2.2 demonstrates a data sequence of 5 dominant data bits followed by a recessive stuff bit. Following this stuff bit is a sequence of 4 more recessive bits, which results in another 5 bit sequence of the same polarity. In accordance with the CAN standard, the sending node must insert yet another (dominant) stuff bit.

7.3 BIT TIMING AND SYNCHRONIZATION

As was explained in *Chapter 7.1 - Bit Coding* the CAN standard uses the Non-Return-to-Zero (NRZ) bit coding, which provides a maximum of data transport capacity, but in turn lacks sufficient means of bit synchronization between sender and receivers in a CAN network.

Bit Stuffing, i.e. the insertion of an additional bit of reversed polarity after a series of bits of the same polarity, provides a higher number of signal edges for synchronization, but, with maximum reliability requirements in mind, Bit Stuffing alone was deemed not quite sufficient.

In order to assure that all receivers in a CAN network read the transmitted frames correctly they are also required to continuously resynchronize the internal time base with the received bit stream. This is accomplished by continuously adjusting the bit sample point during each bit time. The purpose of bit timing synchronization is to coordinate the oscillator frequencies in a CAN network and as a result provide a system wide specified time reference.

7.3.1   BIT SAMPLE POINT

One topic that had not been addressed so far is: When exactly does a receiving CAN node read the bit information?

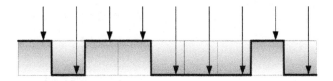

Picture 7.3.1.1: Bit Sample Point

As shown in a random example in picture 7.3.1.1 the bit sample point is located somewhat close to the end of the actual bit time in order to compensate for signal propagation delays in the CAN network plus delays within the actual CAN receiver/transmitter circuits.

Since the CAN standard manages the bus access through bit-wise arbitration, it must be assured that the signal propagation time from sender to receiver and back to the sender must be completed within one bit time.

 *CAN nodes transmitting a message to the bus also monitor the bus and compare the transmitted level bit by bit with the corresponding level on the bus. Consequently, considering the signal propagation time from sender to receiver and back to the sender is mandatory for bit monitoring.*

The determination of the bit sample point, and consequently its positioning, requires an internal detection and simulation of the actual bit time reference.

7.3.2   BIT TIME

In order to determine the exact bit sample point the CAN standard partitions the nominal bit time into four non-overlapping time segments as shown in picture 7.3.2.1.

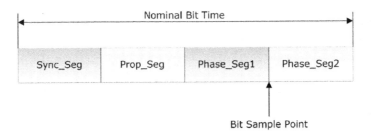

Picture 7.3.2.1: Bit Time Partitioning

The Nominal Bit Time is derived from the Nominal Baud Rate as shown in equation 7.3.2.1:

$$t_B = \frac{1}{BR}$$

tB = Nominal Bit Time

BR = Nominal Baud Rate

Equation 7.3.2.1: Nominal Bit Time

The four non-overlapping time segments used for the partition are (See picture 7.3.2.1):

➤ **Sync_Seg:** Synchronization Segment

This segment is used to synchronize the nodes in a CAN network. A signal edge is expected within this segment. Any deviations, either a premature or delayed signal edge, will be measured and the phase buffer lengths will be adjusted accordingly, which in turn moves the bit sample point (resynchronization).

➤ **Prop_Seg:** Propagation Time Segment

This segment is used to compensate for the physical delay times within the network, such as signal propagation delay and delays within the actual CAN nodes, namely the receiver/transmitter circuits. The segment's length must be twice these delay times to compensate for delays from sender to receiver and back to the sender (See also picture 7.3.2.3).

➤ **Phase_Seg1/2:** Phase Buffer Segment 1/2

These segments are used to compensate for signal edge phase errors. Their length may be adjusted by resynchronization. Phase_Seg1 may be lengthened while Phase_Seg2 is shortened. The length of Phase_Seg2 is programmed to the maximum length of Phase_Seg1 plus the information processing time.

The **Resynchronization Jump Width** defines the upper limit of the amount that is used to lengthen or shorten the phase buffers.

The **Information Processing Time** starts with the bit sample point and is reserved for calculation of the subsequent bit level, for instance, after a bus arbitration loss.

The **Bit Sample Point** is the point in time at which the bus level is read and interpreted as the value of that respective bit. Since the sample point is always at the end of Phase_Seg1, lengthening/shortening the phase buffers will move the actual sample point.

The **Internal Delay Time** of a CAN node is the sum of all asynchronous delays occurring during the transmission and along the reception path, caused by the bit timing logic units of the CAN controller.

$$t_{node} = t_{output} + t_{input}$$

Equation 7.3.2.2: CAN Node Delay Time

In order to assure proper arbitration the following condition must be met:

$$t_{Prop\_Seg} \geq t_{node\_A} + t_{node\_B} + 2 \times t_{bus\_line}$$

Equation 7.3.2.3: Propagation Time Segment Length

For a better understanding of the previously mentioned condition for bus arbitration it is necessary to go step by step, starting with the initiation of a data transfer by a single node[20].

---

[20] ISO 11898-1 only shows a bus arbitration example similar to picture 7.3.2.4, but elaborating comments are very sparse. The Bosch/CiA document does not use any supporting illustrations.

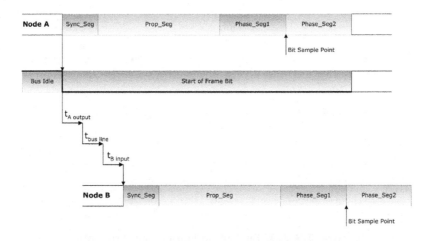

Picture 7.3.2.2: Restart Of Internal Bit Timing

According to the example in picture 7.3.2.2, node A sends an SOF (Start of Frame) bit to the bus, which, after the various delays, is being received by node B. Node B in turn will restart the internal bit timing by resetting its timer, i.e. setting the timer reference to the start of the synchronization segment Sync_Seg. This forces the signal edge to be positioned at the beginning of the synchronization segment.

The detection of a valid signal edge will restart the internal bit timing of a receiving CAN node.

During bus arbitration, however, it may occur that two or more nodes are trying to access the bus virtually at the same time. The use of the Propagation Time Segment Prop_Seg will prevent that all receiving nodes, which are also transmitting nodes at the same time, will reset their internal timing according to the detected signal edge.

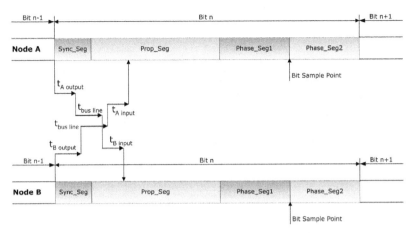

Picture 7.3.2.3: Bit Timing During Bus Arbitration

The example in picture 7.3.2.3 shows a somewhat uncritical timing. Both nodes, A and B, are sending a bit to the bus at exactly the same time. Both will receive the other node's signal edge within the Prop_Seg, i.e. well before the bit sample point. This timing is acceptable for both nodes, meaning there is no action for resynchronization required. At the bit sample point both nodes will read the bus, compare the reading with the transmitted level and proceed according to the rules of bus arbitration (see also *Chapter 6 - Bus Arbitration*).

The next example (see picture 7.3.2.4) demonstrates a more critical timing. Two nodes are trying to access the bus <u>virtually</u> at the same time; in this case node B sends its bit with a slight delay compared to node A, but still within the bit time of node A.

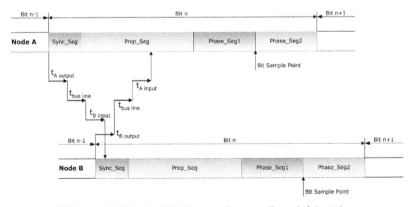

Picture 7.3.2.4: Bit Timing During Bus Arbitration

The length setting of the Propagation Time Segment Prop_Seg is still sufficient to assure proper timing conditions by compensating for the nodes' input/output times plus twice the signal propagation time.

$$t_{\text{Prop\_Seg}} \geq t_{node\_A} + t_{node\_B} + 2 \times t_{bus\_line}$$

Equation 7.3.2.4: Propagation Time Segment Length

7.3.3   BIT TIME PROGRAMMING

The length of the time segments Sync_Seg, Prop_Seg, Phase_Seg1 and Phase_Seg2 are defined (and programmed) in units of time quanta.

A time quantum is a unit of time derived from the oscillator frequency divided by the CAN controller's programmable prescaler, which ranges from 1 to 32. The original time (1/frequency) of the oscillator is defined as the minimum time quantum.

Time Quantum = m x Minimum Time Quantum

where *m* is the prescaler value.

The nominal length of the time segments (without synchronization) is:
- **Sync_Seg:** 1 time quantum.
- **Prop_Seg:** Programmable between 1 and 8 or more[21] time quanta.
- This segment should be programmed to compensate for delays in the CAN network, rounded up to the nearest integer time quantum.
- **Phase_Seg1:** Programmable between 1 and 8 or more[22] time quanta. The actual length may be longer during synchronization.

---

[21] The term "between 1 and 8 or more" is based on the ISO 11898-1 documentation where the exact term is "...1, 2, 3,...,8 or more...". No further details were offered.
[22] The term "between 1 and 8 or more" is based on the ISO 11898-1 documentation where the exact term is "...1, 2, 3,...,8 or more...". No further details were offered.

➤ **Phase_Seg2:** Should be programmed to the maximum of Phase_Seg1 plus the information processing time. The actual length may be shorter during synchronization.

The information processing time is up to 2 time quanta long.

The Resynchronization Jump Width should be programmed between 1 time quantum and the minimum of Phase_Seg1 and 4. In a regular CAN application it is not necessary to program Prop_Seg and Phase_Seg1 separately. It is sufficient to program the sum of both. The total number of time quanta per bit time is also programmable in a range of at least 8 to 25.

The following table shows the recommended bit timing for CAN networks:

Baud Rate	Bit Time	Time quanta per bit	Length of time quantum	Location of sample point
1 MBit/sec	1 µsec	8	125 nsec	6 tq
800 kBit/sec	1.25 µsec	10	125 nsec	8 tq
500 kBit/sec	2 µsec	16	125 nsec	14 tq
250 kBit/sec	4 µsec	16	250 nsec	14 tq
125 kBit/sec	8 µsec	16	500 nsec	14 tq
100 kBit/sec	10 µsec	16	625 nsec	14 tq
50 kBit/sec	20 µsec	16	1.25 µsec	14 tq
20 kBit/sec	50 µsec	16	3.125 µsec	14 tq
10 kBit/sec	100 µsec	16	6.25 µsec	14 tq

Table 7.3.3.1: Bit Timing for CAN Networks

7.3.4   SYNCHRONIZATION

There are two types of synchronization:

➤ **Hard Synchronization** - at the start of a frame (SOF bit)
After a hard synchronization, the internal bit timing of a receiving CAN node will be restarted by resetting the timer, i.e. setting the timer reference to the start of the

synchronization segment Sync_Seg. This forces the signal edge, which has caused the hard synchronization, to be positioned at the beginning of the synchronization segment.

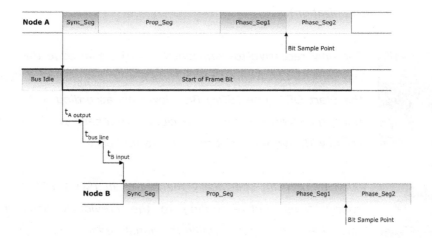

Picture 7.3.4.1: Restart Of Internal Bit Timing

➢ **Bit Resynchronization** - within a frame

Bit resynchronization is accomplished through shortening or lengthening of the phase segments, Phase_Seg1 and Phase_Seg2, in order to correct the position of the bit sample point.

Both types of synchronization are applied according to the following conventions:

➢ There is only one synchronization per one bit time, i.e. between two sample points.

➢ A falling signal edge (recessive to dominant) will only be used for synchronization if the previously detected bus level is different than the level immediately after the edge. This will prevent any reactions due to signal peaks caused by electrical interferences.

➢ A hard synchronization is only initiated through the occurrence of a recessive-to-dominant signal edge during the Interframe Space (intermission field), i.e. when the bus is idle, however, with the exception of the first bit of the Interframe Space.

➢ All other recessive-to-dominant signal edges, following the first two rules, will be used for resynchronization. However, there is an exception where a node sending a dominant bit does not execute bit resynchronization as a result of a recessive-to-dominant signal edge with a positive phase error (see next *Chapter 7.3.5 - Phase Error and Resynchronization*).

The only recessive-to-dominant (falling) signal edge that can occur during the Interframe (Intermission) Field is the first bit of an Overload Frame or the Start Of Frame (SOF) Bit. However, according to the previously listed rules, the Overload Frame is excluded from hard synchronization, because it starts with the first bit of the Interframe Space.

Even though not specifically mentioned in ISO 11898-1 or the Bosch/CiA specifications, but according to the previously listed rules, the only recessive-to-dominant (falling) signal edge that can cause a hard synchronization is the Start Of Frame (SOF) Bit.

7.3.5   PHASE ERROR AND RESYNCHRONIZATION[23]

The phase error of a signal edge is derived from the position of the edge relative to the synchronization segment Sync_Seg, measured in time quanta.

The following assumptions are being applied to explain the phase error and the subsequent bit resynchronization:

➢ The phase error is measured between the detected signal edge and the start of the synchronization segment Sync_Seg (See pictures 7.3.5.2 and 7.3.5.3).[24]

---

[23] The documentation of the phase error of synchronization edges and the following bit synchronization within ISO 11898-1 and the Bosch/CiA standard leave ample room for interpretation. The author has used his best efforts on interpreting this topic according to the available documentation and the statements made therein. The examples used in this book are consistent with the functionality of the phase buffers as described in ISO 11898-1 and the Bosch/CiA documentation.

[24] ISO 11898-1 and the Bosch/CiA documentation refer to the position between the detected signal edge and the Sync_Seg with no reference as to the exact position, i.e. leading or trailing edge of Sync_Seg. The leading edge makes the most sense, since, according to the Bosch/CiA standard, "the effect of a Resynchronization is the same as that of a Hard Synchronization". A hard synchronization forces the leading edge of Sync_Seg to the detected signal edge.

➢ The phase buffers are being adjusted within the same bit time where the edge is detected (Refer to pictures 7.3.5.4 and 7.3.5.5).[25]

➢ After resynchronization within a bit time, which leads to adjusting the phase buffers' length, the phase buffers will be reset to their initial values.[26]

Picture 7.3.5.1 shows an ideal bit timing where the detected signal edges are always located within the synchronization segment.

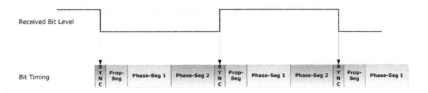

Picture 7.3.5.1: Ideal Bit Timing

However, this example works only in an ideal world. In all reality there will be a phase error between the detected signal edge and the synchronization segment.

The sign of the phase error **e**, negative or positive, is defined as:

➢ e = 0 when the detected signal edge lies within the synchronization segment Sync_Seg of the current bit

➢ e > 0 when the detected signal edge lies after the synchronization segment Sync_Seg and before the sample point of the current bit [27]

---

[25] ISO 11898-1 and the Bosch/CiA documentation do not offer any details.
[26] ISO 11898-1 and the Bosch/CiA documentation do not offer any details.
[27] Both, ISO 11898-1 and the Bosch/CiA standard, use the indistinct term "e > 0 if the edge lies before the sample point".

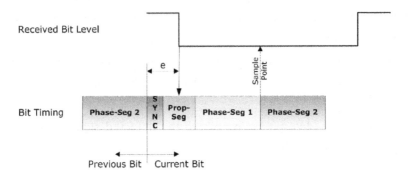

Picture 7.3.5.2: Positive Phase Error

> ➤ e < 0 when the detected signal edge lies before the synchronization segment Sync_Seg of the current bit <u>and</u> after the sample point of the previous bit[28]

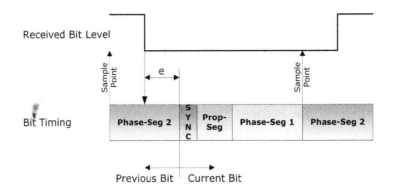

Picture 7.3.5.3: Negative Phase Error

Resynchronization, i.e. the compensation of the phase error, is applied by either lengthening phase buffer 1 or shortening phase buffer 2 according to the sign and amount of the phase error. The effect of adjusting the phase buffer lengths is that first, the bit time will be lengthened or shortened and second, the sample point will be adjusted into the correct position (the actual objective of resynchronization).

---

[28] The Bosch/CiA standard uses the indistinct term "e < 0 if the edge lies after the SAMPLE POINT of the previous bit". ISO 11898-1 only states "e < 0 if the edge lies after the sample point".

Bit resynchronization is applied according to the following rules:

> ➤ The amount of the phase error must be larger than the Resynchronization jump width (SJW).
> ➤ If the phase error is positive, Phase_Seg1 will be lengthened by an amount equal to the resynchronization width (SJW).
> ➤ If the phase error is negative, Phase_Seg2 will be shortened by an amount equal to the resynchronization width (SJW).

 *The calculation of the subsequent bit level must be completed after the end of Phase_Seg2, in case a shortening of Phase_Seg2 results into a length of less than the information processing time.[29]*

 *The effect of resynchronization is the same as that of a hard synchronization[30], i.e. the position of Sync_Seg is being forced to the signal edge.*

 *The maximum length between two transitions in a CAN frame which can be used for bit resynchronization is 29 bit times.[31]*

---

[29] This detail is mentioned only in ISO 11898-1. There is no reference within the Bosch/CiA standard.
[30] As mentioned in the Bosch/CiA standard, but neglected in ISO 11898-1.
[31] As mentioned in the Bosch/CiA standard, but neglected in ISO 11898-1.

Picture 7.3.5.4 demonstrates the compensation of a positive phase error.

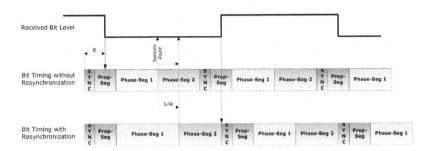

Picture 7.3.5.4: Compensation of Positive Phase Error[32]

In this example, the signal edge is detected after the synchronization segment, but before the sample point of the current bit, which, per definition, will lead to a lengthening of phase buffer 1 by the amount of the resynchronization width SJW.

This will not only move the current sample point into the right position, but also forces the synchronization segment Sync_Seg into the position of the next signal edge.

---

[32] For demonstration purposes, this example uses an equal amount of the phase error and the resynchronization width. Per definition, the amount of the phase error must be larger than the resynchronization width in order to initiate bit resynchronization.

Picture 7.3.5.5 demonstrates the compensation of a negative phase error.

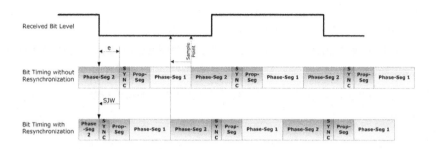

Picture 7.3.5.5: Compensation of Negative Phase Error[33]

In this example, the signal edge is detected before the synchronization segment, but after the sample point of the previous bit, which, per definition, will lead to a shortening of phase buffer 2 by the amount of the resynchronization width SJW.

This will not only move the current sample point into the right position, but also forces the synchronization segment Sync_Seg into the position of the signal edge.

Each resynchronization will compensate the phase error only by the amount of the resynchronization width, which is, per definition, lower than the phase error. As a result there will always be a remaining phase error, which may accumulate over several bit times.[34]

---

[33] For demonstration purposes, this example uses an equal amount of the phase error and the resynchronization width. Per definition, the amount of the phase error must be larger than the resynchronization width in order to initiate bit resynchronization.

[34] This circumstance is neither mentioned in ISO 11898-1 nor the Bosch/CiA specification. The equation to limit the maximum remaining phase error is documented, but no explanation is offered.

7.3.6   OSCILLATOR FREQUENCY TOLERANCE RANGE

The acceptable tolerance range of the actual oscillator frequency around the nominal frequency depends on several factors such as phase buffer 1, phase buffer 2, the resynchronization jump width, and the bit time.

Basically, the maximum acceptable oscillator tolerance range can be described within the following equation:

$$(1-df) \times f_{nom} \leq f_{osc} \leq (1+df) \times f_{nom}$$

f_{osc} Actual Oscillator Frequency

f_{nom} Nominal Oscillator Frequency
df Maximum Tolerance of Oscillator Frequency

Equation 7.3.6.1: Oscillator Frequency Tolerance Range

The maximum frequency tolerance must take the two following equations into consideration, i.e. <u>both</u> must be met.

$$df \leq \frac{(Phase\_Seg1, Phase\_Seg2)_{min}}{2 \times (13 \times t_{bit} - Phase\_Seg2)}$$

df Maximum Tolerance of Oscillator Frequency

t_{bit} Bit Time

Equation 7.3.6.2: Maximum Oscillator Frequency During Error Flag[35]

---

[35] This equation is shown in ISO 11898-1, however, without any elaborating comments or any explanation of the origin of the factors 2 and 13 used in the equation. The Bosch/CiA documentation does not show any equations regarding the oscillator frequency.

Equation 7.3.6.2 applies in case of an error flag (see also *Chapter 4.7.1 - Error Flag*). As shown in picture 7.3.6.1 the actual error flag can be up to 12 bit times long.

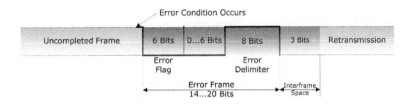

Picture 7.3.6.1: Error Frame

In order to assure correct function of the error counting (see *Chapter 8 -Error Detection and Fault Confinement*) the recessive level following the error flag, i.e. the first bit of the error delimiter, must be received before the sample point of the error frame's 13th bit.

The factor 2 considers the worst case scenario that a sender and receiver may operate at the lower or higher tolerance range, respectively (See equation 7.3.6.3 below).

$$df_{max} = 2 \times df \times f_{nom}$$

df_{max} Maximum Difference between two oscillators
df Maximum Tolerance of Oscillator Frequency
f_{nom} Nominal Oscillator Frequency

Equation 7.3.6.3: Maximum Difference Between Two Oscillators

The next equation explains the relation between the maximum oscillator frequency and the resynchronization jump width.

$$df \leq \frac{SJW}{20 \times t_{bit}}$$

df   Maximum Tolerance of Oscillator Frequency
SJW   Resynchronization Jump Width

t_{bit} Bit Time

Equation 7.3.6.4: Maximum Oscillator Frequency In Relation To SJW[36]

The factor 20 is derived from:

➤ A factor of 2 considers the worst case scenario that a sender and receiver may operate at the lower or higher tolerance range, respectively (See equation 7.3.6.3).

➤ Each resynchronization will compensate the phase error only by the amount of the resynchronization width, which is, per definition, lower than the phase error. As a result there will always be a remaining phase error, which may accumulate over several bit times, but must not exceed the resynchronization jump width SJW within 10 bit times.[37]

---

[36] This equation is shown in ISO 11898-1, however, without any elaborating comments or any explanation of the origin of the factor 20 used in the equation. The Bosch/CiA documentation does not show any equations regarding the oscillator frequency.
[37] This circumstance is neither mentioned in ISO 11898-1 nor the Bosch/CiA specification. The equation to limit the maximum remaining phase error is documented, but no explanation is being offered.

Chapter

8

ERROR DETECTION AND FAULT CONFINEMENT

The CAN standard utilizes a series of error detection mechanisms which contribute to its high level of reliability and error resistance (see *Chapter 8.1 - Error Detection*).

Hear Ye! Hear Ye!

The reliability of CAN has been calculated in a mathematical model. Here is an example using the following parameters and conditions:

- *1 Bit error every 0.7 sec*
- *Baud rate of 500 kBit/sec*
- *Operation of 8 hours/day and 365 days/year*
- *According to this model the Residual Error Probability will be 1 undetected error in 1000 years.*[38]

Fault Confinement guarantees proper network functionality and a continued availability of the data transportation system by adjusting the behavior of defective nodes, even up to a point where a node may remove itself from the network (self-retirement).

---

[38] Source: CAN-in-Automation

8.1 ERROR DETECTION

CAN provides the following procedures to detect errors during a frame transmission:

- ➤ **Bit monitoring**

  Transmitters compare the transmitted level bit by bit with the corresponding level on the bus.

- ➤ **Checksum Check**

  Each CAN data or remote frame includes a 15 bit CRC.

- ➤ **Variable bit stuffing with a stuff width of 5**

  A violation of the bit stuffing rule is considered a "bit stuffing" error.

- ➤ **Frame Check**

  Each transmitting node as well as any receiving node operating within the established specifications will check the consistency of the transmitted frame.

- ➤ **Acknowledge Check**

  All receiving nodes in a CAN network will check the consistency of the received frame and acknowledge a consistent frame or renounce an inconsistent frame. It is the responsibility of the transmitting node to check the acknowledgment (or lack thereof) and send an error frame in case the frame is reported to be corrupt.

8.1.1 BIT MONITORING

CAN nodes transmitting a message to the bus also monitor the bus and compare the transmitted level bit by bit with the corresponding level on the bus. A bit error is detected when the transmitted bit level differs from the monitored bus level.

However, there are exceptions:

➢ A dominant bit on the bus will not lead to a bit error when a recessive bit is transmitted during arbitration.

➢ A dominant bit on the bus will not lead to a bit error when a recessive bit is transmitted during the ACK slot.

➢ A node sending a passive error frame (6 consecutive recessive bits) and detecting a dominant bit will not interpret this as a bit error (see also *Chapter 8.3 - Fault Confinement*).

Bit monitoring not only allows global error detection within the network, but also allows the location of the error source (local error detection).

8.1.2   CHECKSUM CHECK

The 15 bit CRC Segment (CRC = Cyclic Redundancy Code) in a data or remote frame contains the frame check sequence spanning from SOF (Start of Frame), through the arbitration field, control field and data field. Stuffing Bits are not included (see also *Chapter 7.2 - Bit Stuffing*).

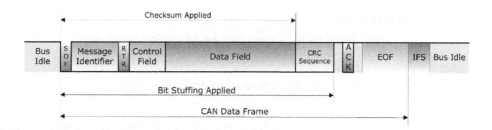

Picture 8.1.2.1: Checksum Application Range

The frame check sequence is derived from a CRC (BCH = Bose-Chaudhuri-Hocquenghem code) best suited for frame lengths of less than 127 bits.[39]

---

[39] More information on the BCH code can be gathered from:
Information Theory, Coding and Cryptography
By Ranjan Bose
ISBN 0-07-048297-7
http://www.tatamcgrawhill.com/digital_solutions/bose/preface.htm

The calculation of the 15 bit checksum is, naturally, somewhat complex and in order to be as correct as possible, the following represents is an excerpt from the Bosch CAN Specification:

"In order to carry out the CRC calculation, the polynomial to be divided shall be specified as the polynomial, the coefficients of which are given by the destuffed bit stream consisting of SOF, arbitration field, control field, data field (if present) and, for the 15 lowest coefficients, by 0. This polynomial shall be divided (the coefficients are calculated modulo-2) by the generator polynomial:

$$X^{15} + X^{14} + X^{10} + X^8 + X^7 + X^4 + X^3 + 1$$

The remainder of this polynomial division is the CRC sequence transmitted over the bus. In order to implement this function, a 15-bit shift register CRC_RG(14 : 0) may be used. If NXTBIT denotes the next bit of the bit stream given by the destuffed bit sequence from SOF until the end of the data field, the CRC sequence shall be calculated as follows.

```
CRC_RG(14 : ) = (0,...,0);            //initialize shift register
REPEAT
        CRCNXT = NXTBIT EXOR CRC_RG(14);
        CRC_RG(14 : 1) = CRC_RG(13 : 0);    //shift left by one position
        CRC_RG(0) = 0;
        IF CRCNXT THEN
                CRC_RG(14 : 0) = CRC_RG(14:0) EXOR (4599hex);
        ENDIF
UNTIL (NXTBIT = [End of data] or there is an error condition).
```

After the transmission/reception of the last bit of the data field, CRC_RG shall contain the CRC sequence."[40]

8.1.3   BIT STUFFING ERROR

A Bit Stuffing error can only occur between SOF (Start Of Frame) bit and (including) the CRC Sequence, since bit stuffing is only applied in these fields (see also *Chapter 7.2 - Bit Stuffing*).

---

[40] Source: CAN Specification Version 2.0
1991, Robert Bosch GmbH

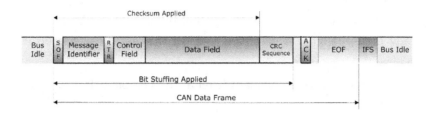

Picture 8.1.3: Bit Stuffing Range

A bit sequence of more then 5 consecutive bits of the same level in a data or remote frame is considered a bit stuffing error.

An error frame intentionally violates the bit stuffing rule, which in turn assures that faulty data or remote frames are destroyed (see also *Chapter 4.7 - Error Frame*).

Another exception to the bit stuffing rule is the overload frame, which uses the same format as the error frame (see *Chapter 4.8 - Overload Frame*).

8.1.4   FRAME CHECK ERROR

The following components of a CAN data or remote frame are considered static fields, since their data level is static (recessive).[41]

> ➢ CRC Delimiter
> ➢ ACK Delimiter
> ➢ End of Frame Field
> ➢ Intermission Field

These components are also used to check the consistency of a data or remote frame. A form error is detected when either of these components contains one or more dominant bits.[42]

---

[41] The ISO 11898-1 and the Bosch/CiA standard refer to the static fields in various chapters, but omit a precise definition.
[42] The ISO 11898-1 and the Bosch/CiA standard refer to "illegal bits", which, in all consequence, can only be dominant bits, since the static fields contain only recessive bits.

However, the exceptions are:

- ➤ When a receiver monitors a dominant level at the last bit of EOF (End of Frame field)
- ➤ When any node monitors a dominant level at the last bit of the error delimiter (see also *Chapter 4.7 - Error Frame*)
- ➤ When any node monitors a dominant level at the last bit of the overload delimiter (see also *Chapter 4.8 - Overload Frame*)

No error will be reported, i.e. no frame error detected, when any of these exceptions occurs.

8.1.5   ACKNOWLEDGEMENT ERROR

The acknowledgement field serves as a confirmation of a successful CRC (checksum) check by the receiving nodes in the network. The message transmitting node monitors the bus and expects a dominant level during the ACK slot. This will be the case when either one of the receiving CAN nodes outputs a dominant level, i.e. acknowledging a successful CRC check (see also *Chapter 4.5 - Message Frame Format*). An ACK Error is detected by a transmitting node in case it does not monitor a dominant bit during the ACK slot.

8.2 ERROR SIGNALING

A damaged frame will be identified and labeled by the transmitting node and any error-free operating receiving node. Defective frames will be aborted and retransmitted according to the CAN recovery procedure. The recovery time, i.e. the time between detecting the error and the possible start of the next frame, is typically between 17 and 23 bit times (length of error frame plus interframe space; see also *Chapter 4.7 - Error Frame*); in cases of a heavily disturbed bus, the recovery time may be up to 23 bit times, provided there are no further errors.

Aborted frames will be automatically retransmitted when the bus is idle again. A retransmitted frame is being handled as any other frame, i.e. it has to re-initiate the arbitration process in order to gain the bus access.

8.3 Fault Confinement

Without the presence of a proper fault confinement method defective CAN nodes would have the potential to disturb the network functionality up to a degree of total ineffectiveness.

The following describes sample scenarios of transmitting and receiving malfunctions that, without fault confinement, would have a disrupting effect on the system performance:

1. **Transmitting Error:**

   A malfunctioning node sends a high-priority (low message ID), but defective frame to the bus. All other functioning nodes in the network would detect and report the error. According to the CAN standard the malfunctioning node would automatically retransmit the same faulty frame over and over again. Any other frame with lower priority would never be able to access the CAN bus.

2. **Receiving Error:**

   A malfunctioning node receives a perfectly good frame, but detects and reports an error. According to the CAN standard the transmitting node would automatically retransmit the frame and the malfunctioning node would report an error over and over again. Just as in the previous scenario, any lower priority frame would not be able to access the CAN bus.

The CAN standard does not consider a so-called "Inhibit Time", which would put a node on hold for a certain time period after the transmission of a message, thus allowing other nodes to access the bus. Higher layer protocols such as CANopen and DeviceNet do provide an Inhibit Time (see picture 8.3.1). However, it is possible to implement the Inhibit Time into a regular CAN application.

Picture 8.3.1: Inhibit Time

While the previously explained scenarios are based on permanent node failures, there might also be cases of sporadic failures, for instance, due to random environmental effects such as electrical disturbances on the bus, etc.

In order to assure system functionality the CAN standard demands that CAN nodes must be able to distinguish sporadic disturbances from permanent failures. Any permanently malfunctioning node must be, first of all, detected (localized) and then logically disconnected from the bus (self-retirement), so that it can neither send nor receive any frames.

The self-retirement of a CAN node will, of course, limit the functionality of the CAN application. The determination of the effect of removing a malfunctioning node from the network and the resulting actions must be application-specific.

To accomplish the ability to distinguish between sporadic and permanent errors, a CAN chip is supplied with two counters, a transmit error counter and a receive error counter. In case of an error, transmitting or receiving, the respective counter will be increased. If frames are sent or received correctly, the respective counter will be decreased.

In terms of increasing or decreasing the counters CAN controllers support a somewhat conservative behavior, which nevertheless contributes to the quest for maximum reliability: The counters are usually increased faster than they are decreased (see also *Chapter 8.3.1 - Error Counting*).

With respect to fault confinement and its objective to adjust the behavior of defective nodes, a node, depending on the error counter value, may operate in different states:

> **Error Active**[43]

Receive <u>and</u> transmit error counter values are less than 128.

An error-active node is a properly working node that participates in the bus communication without restrictions. When an error is detected an error-active node will send an active error flag, which consists of 6 consecutive dominant bits (see also *Chapter 4.7.1 - Error Flag*).

> **Error Passive**

Receive <u>or</u> transmit error counter value is higher than 127.

An error-passive node takes part in the bus communication without restrictions. However, when detecting an error it can only send a passive error flag, which consists of 6 consecutive recessive bits. After a transmission, an error-passive node will wait for a certain time before initiating further transmissions.

Due to the passive error flag, i.e. 6 consecutive recessive bits, a transmitting error-passive node can only report the termination of its own message to the bus, but it cannot destroy any message it received from other nodes.[44]

The detection of an error that causes the transition from error-active to error-passive status is still reported through an active error flag.

An error-passive node will return to error-active status when both, the receive error counter and transmit error counter, are less than or equal to 127.

> **Bus-Off**

Transmitter error counter value is higher than 255.

While in the bus-off state a CAN node will not participate in the bus communication in any way, i.e. it cannot send any frames, ACK, error frames or overload frames.

---

[43] In plain English "Error Active" indicates that the node is working correctly.

[44] The reason of using a passive error flag is neither explained in ISO 11898-1 nor in the Bosch CAN Specification.

Depending on the implementation a CAN node in bus-off state may, however, receive frames.[45]

➢ A recovery from the bus-off state can only be accomplished upon user request, for instance, by resetting the CAN node.

The exact conditions for recovery from bus-off are:
- Both counters, receive error counter and transmit error counter, are set to zero (A hardware reset will do exactly that).
- The node has to undergo a system start-up, it has to wait for 128 occurrences of 11 consecutive recessive bits on the bus.

Picture 8.3.2 demonstrates the 3 node states in terms of counter values and the corresponding node status.

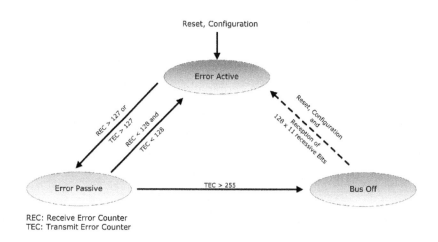

Picture 8.3.2: CAN Node Error Status

The picture also demonstrates the transitions between the node states, however, only the transition between error-active and error-passive is bi-directional. The transition to bus-off cannot lead back to the error-passive status.

___

[45] ISO 11898-1 mentions in chapter 6.15: "In the bus-off state, a node shall neither send nor receive any frames", while in chapter 13.1.4.4 it mentions: "Whether such a node receives frames from the bus depends on the implementation".

A node that had been in bus-off status must accomplish a start-up routine in order to:

➢ Synchronize with other nodes in the network before initiating any transmission. Synchronization is achieved when 11 recessive bits are monitored, which are equivalent to

- ACK delimiter + EOF + Intermission, or
- Error/Overload delimiter + Intermission

➢ Wait for other nodes in the network, however, without the risk of returning to bus-off status in case there is no other node available at the time.

If during system start-up only one node is connected to the network and it transmits any frame, it will not receive an ACK. It will therefore detect an error and repeat the frame. Such a node may become error-passive, but, per definition, may not become bus-off.

An error counter value greater than 96 indicates a heavily disturbed bus.[46] It will benefit any CAN application to check for this condition and provide the proper user feedback.

8.3.1   ERROR COUNTING

The error counters will be increased or decreased according to the following rules:[47]

➢ The receive error counter will be increased by 1 when a receiving node detects an error condition.

---

[46] Source: Bosch CAN Specification.
[47] More than one rule may apply during the duration of a frame.

- Exception: The detected error was a bit error during the transmission of an active error flag or overload flag.

➢ The receive error counter will be increased by 8 when a receiving node monitors a dominant bit directly after sending an error flag.

➢ The transmit error counter will be increased by 8, when the transmitting node sends an error flag.

- Exception 1: The transmitting node is error-passive and detects an ACK error and does not detect a dominant bit while sending a passive error flag.

- Exception 2: A transmitting node sends an error flag due to a bit stuffing error during bus arbitration, where the stuff-bit was sent recessive, but monitored as dominant.

In both exceptions the transmit error counter remains unchanged.

➢ The transmit error counter will be increased by 8 when a transmitting node detects a bit error during sending an active error flag or an overload flag.

➢ The receive error counter will be increased by 8 when a receiving node detects a bit error during sending an active error flag or an overload flag.

➢ Any node will tolerate up to 7 consecutive dominant bits after sending an active error flag, passive error flag or an overload flag. Each transmitting node will increase its transmit counter by 8 and each receiving node will increase its receive error counter by 8 after detecting the 14th consecutive dominant bit[48] or after detecting the 8th dominant bit following a passive error flag, and after each sequence of additional 8 consecutive dominant bits.

---

[48] In case of an active error flag or an overload flag.

➢ After a successful transmission of a frame, i.e. receiving a dominant ACK and no error was reported until the end of the frame (EOF), the transmit error counter will be decreased by 1, unless it was already zero.

➢ The receive error counter will be decreased by 1 under the following conditions:

- The frame was received without error up to the ACK slot.
- Successful sending of the ACK bit.
- The receive error counter value was between 1 and 127.
  If the receive error counter was already at zero it will remain at zero.
  If the receive error counter was greater than 127 it will be set to a value between 119 and 127.

Chapter

9

PHYSICAL LAYER

The ISO/OSI Reference Model specifies 7 levels beginning with the physical connection up to the actual user application, i.e. the Application Layer.[49]

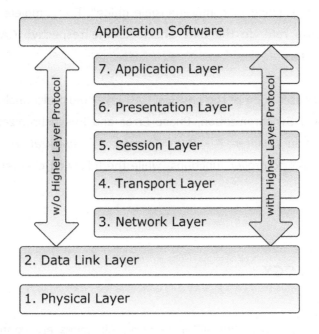

Picture 9.1: ISO/OSI 7 Layer Reference Model

---

[49] For more information on the OSI Reference Model refer to:
CertificationZone.com OSI Reference Model Pocket Guide
by Howard C. Berkowitz - ISBN: 1890911143

The standard CAN implementation bypasses the connection between the Data Link Layer and the Application Layer in order to save on valuable memory resources by minimizing the overhead and, as a result, gaining performance as needed for embedded solutions with limited resources. After all, all layers above the Data Link Layer require additional software resources (higher layer protocols).

The CAN Data Link Layer is, to a certain degree, documented in the Bosch CAN Specification Version 2.0 and the ISO 11898-1 Standard. A documentation of the CAN Physical Layer is available through two documents:

1. **ISO 11898-2** concentrates mainly on the physical signals on the CAN bus.

2. **CiA Draft Standard DS-102** recommends hardware connections and baud rates.[50]

The following sections are designed to provide an overview of the CAN Physical Layer, however, in the sense of being a "comprehensible guide". For complete details on the exact CAN bus signals please refer to the data sheets of the respective CAN Transceivers (See *Chapter 9.5 - Bus Connection*).

In all consequence, a description of the physical CAN layer must also include topics such as Bit Coding, Bit Timing and Synchronization, Phase Error and Resynchronization, etc., which has already been detailed in *Chapter 7 - Data Transfer Synchronization*. These topics relate, however, to internal CAN controller functions, while the following chapters describe "external" topics.

9.1 BUS TOPOLOGY

Picture 9.1.1 demonstrates a sample CAN network. All nodes are connected by two wires, CAN_H and CAN_L. The bus line is terminated by resistors, which are typically 120 Ω and are

---

[50] DS-102 is a mere 5 page document that, besides the recommended pin assignment of a CAN connector and CAN baud rates, contains primarily references to documents such as the Bosch CAN Specification, ISO 11898, and even a meeting protocol, that is not available anymore.

necessary to suppress any electrical reflections on the bus. The termination resistors should always be connected at both ends of the bus; they should never be physically attached to a CAN node, because the bus would lose proper termination in case this specific node is being removed.

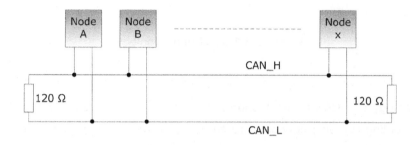

Picture 9.1.1: Bus Topology

CAN_L and CAN_H represent the physical connection between CAN nodes; they do not represent actual voltage levels. CAN_H will be at (nominal) 3.5 V during a dominant bit, while CAN_L will be at 1.5 V, which makes CAN_H the higher voltage. This may be the reason the creators of the CAN standard chose to use this terminology.

Hear Ye! Hear Ye!

According to ISO 11898-2 the termination resistor should be in the range of 100...130 Ω, but should typically be at 120 Ω, with a minimum power dissipation of 220 mWatts. Deviations from the nominal value of 120 Ω are possible, depending on the actual bus topology and the baud rate. As a rule of thumb, the lower the termination resistor the lower is the number of possible nodes in the network.

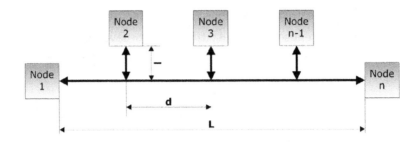

Picture 9.1.2: Wiring Topology

The wiring topology of a CAN network should be as straight as possible, i.e. using short cable lengths and avoiding complex network structures (even though almost any network structure is possible under CAN).

As described in more detail in *Chapter 9.6 - Maximum Bus Length* the maximum bus length L depends on the used baud rate. Table 9.1.1 shows some network topology parameters at the maximum baud rate of 1 MBit/sec.

Parameter	Maximum Length [ft] / [m]
L - Bus Length	120 / 40
I - Cable Stub Length	1 / 0.3
d - Node Distance	120 /40

Table 9.1.1: Network Topology Parameters at 1 MBit/sec

The bus length can be extended significantly at lower baud rates (see also *Chapter 9.6 - Maximum Bus Length*).

9.2 BUS MEDIUM

According to specification the CAN bus medium must support two logical states: Recessive and dominant.

A CAN controller with its TTL output uses an additional line driver (transceiver) to provide the standard CAN level (For more details see *Chapter 9.5 - Bus Connection*). The dominant level (TTL = 0V) always overrides a recessive level (TTL = 5V), which is important especially during bus arbitration. As demonstrated in picture 9.2.1 the CAN bus level will be dominant in case any number of nodes in the network output a dominant level. The CAN bus level will only be recessive when all nodes in the network output a recessive level.

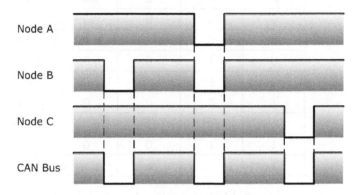

Picture 9.2.1: CAN Node Output and Bus Level

An equivalent from some electronics basics will explain the relationship between node output and the resulting bus level as shown in picture 9.2.2.

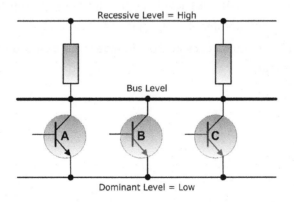

Picture 9.2.2: Open Collector Principle on a CAN bus

This example uses three nodes in a CAN network, in this case represented by three transistors in open-collector ("Wired And") configuration. The bus level will be at low level (dominant) in case any number of transistors in the network output a dominant level. The bus level will only be at high level (recessive) when all transistors in the network output a recessive level.

Node			
A	B	C	Bus
0	0	0	0
0	0	1	0
0	1	0	0
0	1	1	0
1	0	0	0
1	0	1	0
1	1	0	0
1	1	1	1

Table 9.2.1: Wired And

9.4 BUS SIGNAL LEVEL

As shown in picture 9.4.1 the CAN bus level ranges normally (Common-Mode-Voltage = 0V) between 1.5 (CAN_L during dominant bit) and 3.5 Volts (CAN_H during dominant bit). However, the actual signal status, recessive or dominant, is based on the differential voltage V_{diff} between CAN_H and CAN_L.

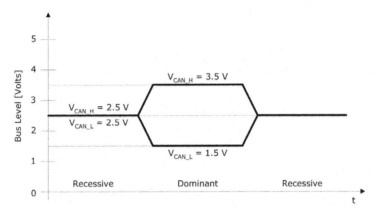

Picture 9.4.1: CAN Bus Level[51]

$$V_{diff} = V_{CAN\_H} - V_{CAN\_L}$$

Equation 9.4.1: Differential Voltage

V_{diff} will be 2V during a dominant bit and 0V during a recessive bit.

During bus arbitration several CAN nodes may transmit a dominant bit simultaneously to the bus. In this case V_{diff} will exceed the nominal level as seen during single operation, i.e. when the bus is driven by only one node.

The advantage of using a differential voltage between CAN_H and CAN_L lies in its resistance to electromagnetic interferences (EMI). Any EMI will affect both wires in the same way, but the differential voltage level will remain constant.

9.5 BUS CONNECTION

In order to connect to the physical CAN bus, a CAN controller with its TTL output uses an additional line driver (transceiver) to provide the standard CAN level (See picture 9.5.1).

---

[51] ISO 11898-2 on page 4 – Figure 2 shows a similar, however, in the humble opinion of the author, misleading picture representing the physical bit level. It can only be assumed that the picture refers to the bus level during bus arbitration, but, as usual, elaborating comments have been omitted.

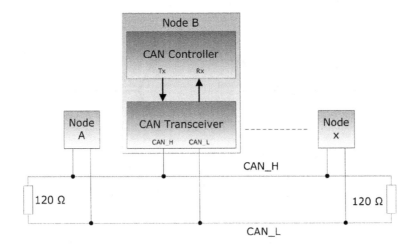

Picture 9.5.1: CAN Controller and Transceiver

The transceiver converts the standard TTL level (in some cases 3 V instead of the standard 5 V) into a differential voltage, i.e. the CAN bus level (See picture 9.4.1) and vice versa.

Picture 9.5.2 demonstrates both signals, TTL and CAN bus.

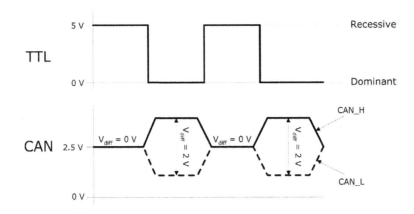

Picture 9.5.2: Physical Bit Representation

The actual signal status, recessive or dominant, is based on the differential voltage V_{diff} between CAN_H and CAN_L.

$$V_{diff} = V_{CAN\_H} - V_{CAN\_L}$$

Equation 9.4.1: Differential Voltage

V_{diff} will be 2V during a dominant bit and 0V during a recessive bit.

9.6 MAXIMUM BUS LENGTH

The maximum bus length of a CAN network depends on various factors, but most crucially on the used baud rate as demonstrated in picture 9.6.1:

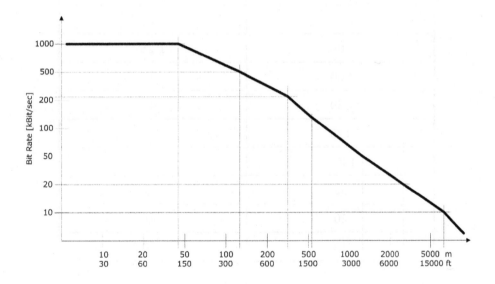

Picture 9.6.1: Maximum Bus Length

As a rule of thumb, for bus lengths greater than 100 m or 300 ft, the product of bus length and baud rate should not exceed 60.

The reason for the limited bus length at higher baud rates lies in the bus latency time, i.e. the time it takes for a signal to travel through the entire bus and back (see also *Chapter 7.3.2 - Bit*

Time). The bus latency time is crucial especially during bus arbitration, but also for the bit monitoring of a node.

Since the CAN standard manages the bus access through bit-wise arbitration, it must be assured that the signal propagation time from sender to receiver and back to the sender must be completed within one bit time.

CAN nodes transmitting a message to the bus also monitor the bus (bit monitoring) and compare the transmitted level bit by bit with the corresponding level on the bus. Consequently, considering the signal propagation time from sender to receiver and back to the sender is mandatory for bit monitoring.

The CiA Draft Standard DS-102 recommends the following baud rates:

Bit Rate [kBit/sec]	Nominal Bit Time [µsec]
1000	1
800	1.25
500	2
250	4
125	8
100[52]	10
50	20
20	50
10	100

Table 9.6.1: Recommended Baud Rates According to DS-102

---

[52] DS-102 remarks: "Not recommended for new developments" with no further explanation.

9.7 WIRING AND CONNECTORS

CAN is not very demanding in terms of cable requirements. Due to its high protection against EMI the use of a twisted-pair wiring will be sufficient. However, for the use in harsh electrical environments and especially at maximum baud rate, the use of a shielded cable is recommended.

Even though CAN is generally used as a two-wire network, it may be necessary in some cases to connect the CAN Ground signal. The grounding of the shielding on one side of the connection is mandatory to assure effectiveness of the shielding.

The CiA DS-102 document recommends the use of a 9-pin D-Sub connector according to DIN 41652 or the corresponding international standard.

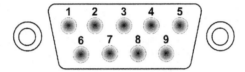

Picture 9.7.1: Pin Numbers of D-Sub Connector – Male

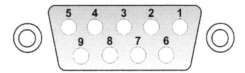

Picture 9.7.2: Pin Numbers of D-Sub Connector – Female

Pin	Signal	Description
1	-	Reserved
2	CAN_L	CAN_L bus line (dominant low)
3	CAN_GND	CAN Ground
4	-	Reserved
5	CAN_SHLD	Optional CAN shield
6	GND	Optional CAN Ground
7	CAN_H	CAN_H bus line (dominant high)
8	-	Reserved (error line)
9	CAN_V+	Optional CAN external positive supply[53]

Table 9.7.1: Pin Assignment

[53] DS-201 mentions "The electrical parameters for pin 9 (V+) refer to the proposal of the working group "Physical Layer". They are not yet agreed upon by the General Assembly of CAN in Automation".

Chapter 110

SUMMARY

As was detailed in this *Comprehensible Guide*, Controller Area Network is superior to any other field-bus system in regards to low cost, the ability to function in a difficult electrical environment, a high degree of real time capability, excellent error detection and fault confinement capabilities and, almost contradictive to the previously mentioned features, ease of use.

The ingenious design of CAN is one of the deciding factors that will guarantee a long life span of the technology, despite the emergence of newer technologies claiming better performance.

During the years, since the publication of the CAN standard, there has been the quest to create and establish better and faster field bus technologies, but none of them has managed to replace CAN as of yet. The development of higher layer protocols opened the way into industrial automation, even highly complex and demanding tasks such as motion control.

CANopen, for instance, is an adequate technology to handle in excess of 90% of all motion control tasks in the automation industry. This is guaranteed by the principle of distributed control. The actual crunching work is accomplished by the nodes in the network, in case of motion control, the motion controller. For the vast majority of industrial automation tasks, CANopen is quite able to provide the communication means between nodes even up to real-time synchronization.

Currently there are activities to promote field bus technologies based on Ethernet, which definitely provide higher performance in regards to inter-node communication and they may have a chance to replace CAN in the long run. Higher performance is definitely the answer to, for instance, high-speed high-precision robotics, but such demanding automation tasks cannot be considered daily business for the average automation engineer.

The promoters of Ethernet-based field bus technologies do a great job explaining the technical advantages, but they fall short when it comes to explaining the considerable resources needed to integrate their technology, may it be the implementation of non-standard hardware or (considerable) software license fees.

As long as new technologies are not able to match the price over performance ratio of CAN and its higher layer protocols, they will not manage to replace Controller Area Network as the "best-choice" field bus technology for industrial automation.

Appendix A - References

/1/

International Standard ISO 11898-1

First edition 2003-12-01

Road vehicles – Controller area network (CAN) –

Part 1: Data link layer and physical signaling

Reference number ISO 11898-1:2003(E)

/2/

International Standard ISO 11898-2

First edition 2003-12-01

Road vehicles – Controller area network (CAN) –

Part 2: High-speed medium access unit

Reference number ISO 11898-2:2003(E)

/3/

ROBERT BOSCH GmbH

CAN Specification

Version 2.0

1991, Robert Bosch GmbH, Postfach 50, D-7000 Stuttgard 1

/4/

CiA CAN in Automation

CAN Specification, Part A

/5/

CiA CAN in Automation

CAN Specification, Part B

/6/

CiA CAN in Automation

The CAN physical layer

/7/

CiA CAN in Automation

CiA Draft Standard 102 Version 2.0

CAN Physical Layer for Industrial Applications

20 April 1994

Two Wire Differential Transmission

/8/

Pfeiffer, Olaf and Andrew Ayre, Christian Keydel

Embedded Networking with CAN and CANopen

2003, RTC Books

/9/

Etschberger, Konrad

Controller Area Network

2000, IXXAT Automation

/10/

Lawrenz, Wolfhard

CAN Controller Area Network, Grundlagen und Praxis

2000, Huethig Verlag

/11/

Jack Shandle

CAN: Network for Thousands of Applications Outside Automotive

http://www.techonline.com

/12/

Peter Bagschick

An Introduction to CAN

2000, I+ME ACTIA GmbH, Germany

/13/

Controller Area Network – A Serial Bus System – Not Just For Vehicles

esd gmbh, Hannover, Germany

/14/

CiA CAN in Automation

CANopen – Cabling and Connector Pin Assignment

CiA Draft Recommendation DR-303-1

Version 1.0 – October 10, 1999

Index

SOF, 36, 43, 45, 75, 77

SRR, 56

standard format, 53

Standard Format, 55

Start of Frame, 43, 45

start-up routine, 127

Stuff Bit, 96

Substitute Remote Request, 56

super positioning, 61, 68

superposition, 58

Sync_Seg, 101, 103, 105, 108, 109

Synchronization, 99, 106

synchronization segment, 103

Synchronization Segment, 101

termination resistors, 132

time quantum, 105

transceiver, 135, 137

Transceivers, 132

Transmission Times, 71

transmit error counter, 124, 128

Transmitter error counter, 125

Transmitting Error, 60, 123

V_{diff}, 136

Wired And, 34, 88, 136

Wiring, 141

Wiring Topology, 134

Lightning Source UK Ltd.
Milton Keynes UK
UKOW05f2357060716

277862UK00013B/611/P